Miss M. G. Shaw.

Copyhold

Nr Haslemere.

# A Countrywoman's Journal

## THE SKETCHBOOKS OF A
## PASSIONATE NATURALIST

*Margaret Shaw in Japanese style, circa 1918.*

# A Countrywoman's Journal

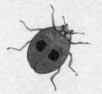

## THE SKETCHBOOKS OF A PASSIONATE NATURALIST

*Margaret Shaw*

WITH AN INTRODUCTION BY PEGGY VANCE
FORMERLY A CURATOR OF DESIGN, PRINTS AND DRAWINGS AT THE
VICTORIA & ALBERT MUSEUM, LONDON

APOLLO PUBLISHING

Picture credit, p.18: Craig Knowles/Country Life Library.

Published by Apollo Publishing Ltd, 17 Langbourne Mansions, Highgate, London N6 6PR.

A copy of the British Library Cataloguing in Publication Data for this title
is available from the British Library.

First printing 2002.
Printed in Spain.

ISBN 0 9535784 9 6

Book designer: David Fordham.
Natural history consultant and indexer: Jonathan Elphick.

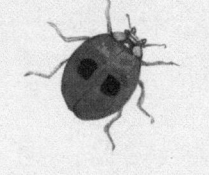

# CONTENTS

*Note to reader*
This book is a facsimile of
Margaret Shaw's sketchbooks,
so the omissions and imperfections
of the original have been retained.

*Hand-tinted photograph of Margaret Shaw,* circa *1910.*

# INTRODUCTION

*"With fascinating observations and a meticulous hand,
Margaret Shaw created a remarkable record of English wildlife
in the 1920s."*

COUNTRY LIFE

One Spring afternoon, when clearing out old papers from a drawer, Sussex farmer Reg Pritchard found a pair of smallish sketchbooks, beautifully bound in coarse linen. Despite the fierce sea breezes and salt mists of many coastal winters, they seemed to be in perfect condition, neither warped nor marked. Gently removing the old tie-bands, he opened the sketchbooks – and what he saw was quite incredible.

Reg had stumbled upon the discovery of a lifetime. Brilliant butterflies, songbirds and seabirds, plants and seeds, bees and bugs teemed across the pages, each captured with the delicacy of a pressed flower. Here was Margaret Shaw's great secret, never revealed to him in the fifteen years they had shared a home.

*Margaret's mother, Grace, notes the
details of her daughter's birth: at
5.30 am on Tuesday 6th July 1886.
She weighed 9lbs, had dark hair and
eyes, and was christened on 3rd August.*

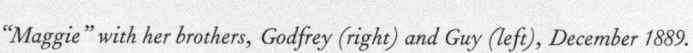

*"Maggie" with her brothers, Godfrey (right) and Guy (left), December 1889.*

To Reg Margaret was "Auntie", a kindly friend thirty years his senior, and a countrywoman. In fact, Margaret Grace Shaw, photographed as a child by the Queen's photographer and a pupil at the select Cheltenham Ladies' College, had been born into a family of wealthy industrialists. Her grandfather, Matthew T. Shaw, owned the eponymous company, which had wharves and ironworks on the Isle of Dogs in East London. Around 1886, when Margaret was born, the increasing industrialisation of Victorian Britain led to an unprecedented demand for iron structures on a grand scale, and money poured into the family coffers. The Shaws bought yachts, travelled widely abroad, and, at the turn of the century, owned some of the earliest motor cars in Britain.

### An Idyllic Childhood

With her two older brothers, Godfrey and Guy, Margaret was very much a tomboy, swimming, riding and playing cricket to pass the long hot afternoons of summer. Their father, Harry, often joined their games, and Margaret adored him. In May 1902, when climbing a tree, she lost her footing and ended up, as her diary records, "hung elegantly" from a branch by the skirt of her gym dress:

*I heard a tremendous clapping from father who said that he would come
and photograph me if I did it again.*

8

*Margaret aged about eight, posed by Walery, "Photographer to the Queen".*

It would seem that Margaret's mother, Grace – the "G.M.S." so often mentioned in the journals that are reproduced here – was equally loving and playful. Margaret records her mother's tendernesses, such as giving her not one but two bars of chocolate before her return to school. Margaret was always sad to leave her parents and, on Tuesday 25th June 1901, she noted:

> *Mother went this morning as I went to college. It was horrid to part*
> *after such a happy time... I have a lovely picture of mother and*
> *father for my birthday.*

*"M.G.S. [Margaret] taking a flat header."*

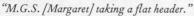

*Bathing in the Hamble river.*

*"M.G.S. being hauled in."*

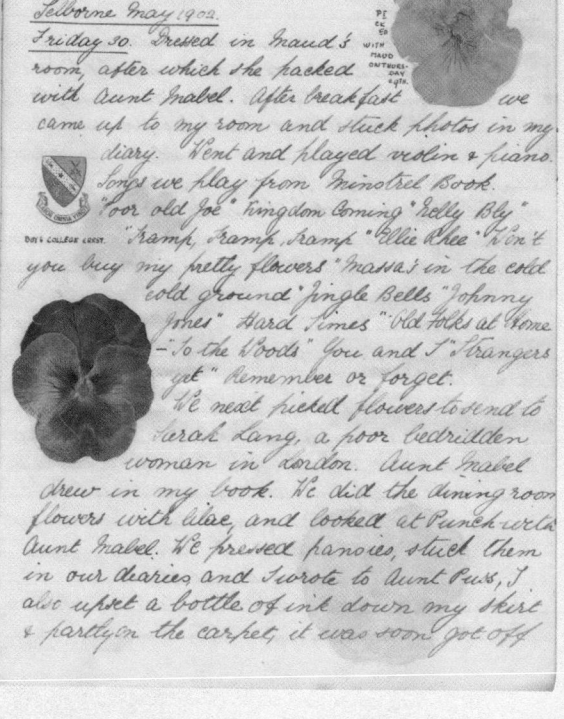

*Selborne May 1902.*

*Thursday 29* Violin & Piano while Mother was in the kitchen. Before breakfast we picked our flowers for Mrs Williams & Aunt Elsie. We put them in water till about 10p when we packed them up to go by the evening post. We searched in the bake house after lunch for the croquet balls which we found after a long hunt. We also found a lot of old books on trials from "Henry IV to Queen Anne." I have now put them in my cupboard to take care of them. Father has given me a little box for nails & tools etc which I have got in my room. We also pressed pansies in the Afternoon. We went to Legs to get Postal Orders and to Maxwells for Buttons and elastic. After tea we wrote our Diaries. After Dinner we

played khanhoo until about 10p, then we went to bed. Heard that I am to return to college on June 6th.

*Selborne May 1902.*

*Friday 30.* Dressed in Maud's room, after which she packed with Aunt Mabel. After breakfast we came up to my room and stuck photos in my diary. Went and played violin & piano. Songs we play from Minstrel Book. "Poor old Joe" "Kingdom Coming" "Nelly Bly" "Tramp, Tramp, Tramp" "Ellie Rhee" "Won't you buy my pretty flowers" "Massa's in the cold cold ground" "Jingle Bells" "Johnny Jones" "Hard Times" "Old Folks at Home" "To the Woods" "You and I" "Strangers yet" "Remember or forget". We next picked flowers to send to Sarah Lang, a poor bedridden woman in London. Aunt Mabel drew in my book. We did the dining room flowers with lilac, and looked at Punch with Aunt Mabel. We pressed pansies, stuck them in our diaries and wrote to Aunt Puss, I also upset a bottle of ink down my skirt & partly on the carpet, it was soon got off

*Margaret's early diary with pressed pansies, picked on the morning of Thursday 29th May 1902.*

### THE GILBERT WHITE CONNECTION

At fifteen Margaret seemed a most contented girl, well educated and in the heart of a loving family. In May 1901 the Shaws had moved from a sizeable country house, St Leonard's Grange in Beaulieu, to Selborne, thirty miles to the north-east, where they had bought The Wakes, a grand residence in which, between 1728 and 1793, the naturalist, the Rev. Gilbert White, had lived and worked. It is now a well-known museum. Reg Pritchard is in no doubt that Margaret was profoundly influenced by the author of the famous *Natural History and Antiquities of Selborne*

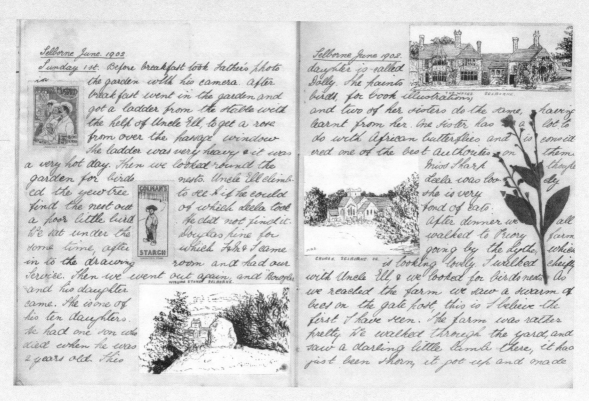

*Diary entries from June 1902 relating to the Shaws' move to The Wakes, Selborne.*

On moving into The Wakes her childhood diary blossoms with pressed pansies and wildflowers, and Saturday 31st May 1902 found her copying directly from Gilbert White:

> *After breakfast drew picture (& inked) of "The Wakes" from*
> *G. White's book, in my Album.*

### A SCHOLAR AND AN ARTIST

Margaret was an able student, ranked third in her class and top in Euclid studies; nevertheless, in keeping with a young lady's syllabus of the time, she spent much of the school day sketching and painting. Classes in perspective, "heads" and drawing were complemented by her own passion for nature, and the observations in the diary of her youth sound remarkably like those of her later journals:

> *… we looked for birds' nests. As we reached the farm we saw a*
> *swarm of bees on the gate post, this is I believe the first I have seen.*
> *The farm was rather pretty. We walked through the yard and saw a*
> *darling little lamb there, it had just been shorn…*
>
> *(JUNE 1902)*

11

*Margaret with Barney, 1912.*

### COMPASSION

Here already is the detail and tenderness that infuses all Margaret Shaw's writings. She cherished animals of all kinds, and her journals repeatedly bear witness to her efforts to protect even the smallest creatures. Aged forty she was no less compassionate than at fifteen. On 5th November 1926 she noted:

> *A Small Tortoiseshell Butterfly flew round our heads at breakfast,*
> *and finally alighted on the floor, where I was only just in time to*
> *rescue it from the cats. I carried it to my South window, where it*
> *sunned itself all day, wandering up and down the panes, with*
> *widespread wings. Each time I attempted to let it out, it folded its*
> *wings tightly and refused to move, so I let it stay in the warm.*

Polly the parrot, Algy the goat, Sally the donkey, Barney the dog and Nicco the cat – the latter much chastised for his murderous ways – were just some of the much-photographed pets on which Margaret lavished her affections over the years. Her concern for animals suggests that Margaret would have been a doting mother, but she never married, and, to Reg Pritchard's knowledge, was never courted. Her maternal instincts were directed instead towards her young cousins, Norah and Mary, who came to live with Margaret in the early 1930s, and whom she treated like daughters, allowing them many privileges.

### THE STABLES

Mary was keen on riding, so lessons were organised with Miss Somerville, who owned a riding school in Haslemere. When, in the mid 1940s, the school came up for sale, Margaret Shaw very generously bought it for Mary, and farmer Reg Pritchard, who lived nearby, was invaluable in helping run the fledgling business.

*Margaret riding with Barney in her arms*, circa *1912*.

### A PURPOSE IN LIFE

Reg, who had struggled desperately to make ends meet during the devastating depression in farming, was run off his feet keeping his farm going, helping with the stable and trying to look after his retarded brother. Seeing his dedication – and his exhaustion owing to the illness and recent death of his mother – Margaret Shaw made an extraordinary offer: to keep house for him and work on the farm. So it was that Reg became her adopted "nephew" and in 1949, aged sixty-three, "Auntie Shaw" moved into the farmhouse that was attached to Reg's farm, near Haslemere.

By that time Margaret had lost her brother Godfrey (who had been killed in India), her parents, and latterly Norah, whose unexpected death she had taken extremely badly. Clearly, with no occupation, so much personal grief to bear and old age looming, Margaret was keen to find a place and a purpose for the final chapter of her life.

*Algy the goat and Sally the donkey with Margaret and family friend*
*Mrs Curtis, summer 1910.*

### COUNTRY LADY TO COUNTRYWOMAN

The transition was nonetheless dramatic. How many women of Margaret Shaw's class and background would have been adaptable enough to swap the life of a privileged country lady for that of a toiling countrywoman? In place of extensive travels, visits to the opera, entertaining and passing the time with literature and games, from 1949, at Reg's farm, Margaret made up the workers' pay packets, helped keep the books, collected the eggs, cared for Reg's brother, and worked ceaselessly for the benefit of the farm.

### CLUES IN THE JOURNALS

Margaret's journals of the 1920s, here reproduced in facsimile, were completed long before this transformation, but in many ways anticipate it. In undertaking the diaries Margaret set herself a daunting challenge. Watercolour is well known to be the most unforgiving medium – blotches cannot be erased or mistakes corrected – and, with great daring and dedication, Margaret chose to paint her finely executed images directly into the sketchbooks. Each page had to be perfect or the book would be ruined.

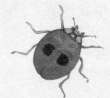

"The House by the side of the road"

When stern reality your golden day-dream shatters,
And life's clouds loom dark and cold above,
You'll wake to find the only thing that really matters
Is the happiness of those you love.

M.G.S.

*A sombre verse, illustrated by Margaret in July 1943.*

## Watching and Painting

Had Margaret been producing quick sketches, she could have worked directly from life, but with many of the subjects she chose to illustrate, she would have had only brief sightings. She needed to make a quick identification and then either paint from memory or use a book illustration as an aide-memoire. She was certainly well read in natural history, but looking up, identifying and copying so many different creatures would have required tireless dedication, especially at a time when there was little colour reference available.

There is no snobbery in the journals. While it is clear from the various locations in which she worked – including Scotland, Wales, France and Italy – that Margaret had wonderful opportunities for travel and leisure, she was as careful in the painting of a common daisy as in the depiction of more rare and exotic discoveries.

## The Animal World

Where Margaret's early diary hummed with people, in the later journals humans are barely in evidence. Margaret's mother and father appear infrequently as "G.M.S." and "H.T.S.", and then only to kill a wasp or feed a bird. The journals are instead peopled by animals; "Mr Sparrow" and "Mr Nuthatch" are spotted on the 25th March 1928 and "Mr G.S.W." – Great Spotted Woodpecker – and his daughter on 9th July of that year. So exclusively does Margaret focus on nature that even the Christmas period goes unremarked, save for the making each year of a tree decorated with food for the birds.

### FREEDOM OF EXPRESSION

In her journals Margaret could escape the strictures of class and society. The animals are her *dramatis personae*, whose antics she watches day by day and records in detail. On 6th August 1927 she observes a confrontation:

> *This morning a wasp got entangled in a spider's web on my*
> *window. The spider darted out, but was afraid to venture too near,*
> *and the next moment the wasp had freed itself and flown away.*
> *The spider retired discomfited.*

There is no pretension in the writing. With the instincts of a true naturalist, she notes down whatever she finds interesting, including more unusual animal behaviours. On 19th July 1927 she was by Dunnet Head lighthouse in the north of Scotland, watching the seabirds:

> *I saw a Lesser Black Backed Gull, the lighthouse man told us they*
> *are regular thieves, and go round turning other birds off their eggs.*
> *As a rule the eggs never fall off the ledges they are laid on, being*
> *shaped so that they only revolve but never roll, but he has seen the*
> *sitting bird pull the egg off the rock with her when attacked by the*
> *L. Black Backed Gull.*

Nowhere are the journals a dry record; throughout they are infused with an infectious enthusiasm. Every sun-dappled day and starlit night is celebrated, and Margaret has a warm descriptive voice that makes for an evocative read:

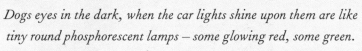

*Great Tits were very busy climbing about the dejected rose bushes.*

*(12TH NOVEMBER 1927)*

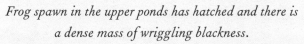

*Dogs eyes in the dark, when the car lights shine upon them are like tiny round phosphorescent lamps – some glowing red, some green.*

*(16TH DECEMBER 1927)*

*Frog spawn in the upper ponds has hatched and there is a dense mass of wriggling blackness.*

*(18TH MARCH 1928)*

## END OF AN ERA

In Shaw's bucolic world the eaves swarm with House Martins, elm trees still grow tall, and the hedgerows are full of "quarrelsome, noisy wrens". What she so poignantly captures is the last of a Britain unspoiled by prairie fields and intensive crop spraying. Here is the country as we would wish it today – fertile, varied and picturesque.

Margaret had an eye for landscape in all weathers and colours: "a glorious sunrise" in Sussex; "a slight fog" in London; and "sullen skies with angry clouds" in the Highlands of Scotland. Watercolour vignettes in her journals capture the most attractive of these scenes. A keen photographer, Margaret often made the landscape her subject, composing images that are strikingly professional.

*Margaret at home in West Sussex, September 1968.*

17

Margaret Shaw was an artist, a naturalist and a writer, but equally she was an inspired and witty designer. Each page of the journal is carefully laid out, and in places Margaret reveals an almost modern design sensibility. Pleasing visual conceits enliven many of the pages: on 17th March 1927 the starlings rise up in a great arc, scattering the text; heavy rain pours right through 1st July 1927, "The wettest day of the year"; and autumn leaves fall across a whole page, from 16th to 20th October 1927.

In everything she did Margaret was creative. Whether painting, embroidering or cooking, she was a perfectionist, always trying to do her best and make the most of her materials. Margaret shared Reg's love of labour and, on Reg's mother's death, helped Reg build his farm into a business so successful that, by September 1955, Reg and Margaret were able to retire to a four-acre seaside estate in West Sussex. Now in his eighties, Reg recalls the contentment he and Margaret found in each other's company:

> *She worked very hard, but she found happiness again. In fact we*
> *were both extremely content. I think we shared the belief that there*
> *was only one way to do a job: perfectly.*

For Margaret it was the ideal retirement, free from worldly cares, at one with the land and the sea, and in a newly minted family: Reg and the wildlife around them. The Margaret Shaw of *A Countrywoman's Journal* had found her natural home.

*Reg Pritchard today, with produce from his kitchen garden.*

# THE
# FIRST JOURNAL

22ND OCTOBER 1926

TO

31ST DECEMBER 1927

*Portrait of Margaret by The London Stereoscopic Company, "photographers to Her late Majesty Queen Victoria", taken on 17th October 1902.*

# Fernhurst Sussex    October 22nd 1926.

A glorious day for late October. The garden is still quite gay with flowers, Dahlias, Chrysanthemums, Stock. Anthrinums, Roses and even a few geraniums and lobelias in full bloom. We drove through Cowdray Park this afternoon, I have never seen it looking more beautiful – The Beeches were in their full glory of autumn tints, with carpets of red fallen leaves at their mossy, spreading, half exposed roots. On every hand were deer, many lying quite close to the road. One big one had chosen a leafy hollow for his bed, and only his horned head and neck were visible, looking for all the world like a fallen branch. I noticed very few birds about. As we came home the sun was dipping into a great bank of billowy grey clouds, edged with gold, and later the whole sky became suffused with delicate pink, overlaid with soft mauve grey clouds.

## October 25th

A Tortoiseshell butterfly has hung itself up to sleep on the ceiling in a corner of my dressingroom. As it is folded up, it is difficult to tell whether it is a Large or a Small one, the latter should have two white spots, one of which is placed close to the tip of each of the front pair of wings – The Large has no white spots at all. I had one of these butterflies in my bedroom all last winter, and on warm sunny days he sometimes came to life and fluttered about in the windows some- windows fed. I ago, but Missel thrush Birds are beginning to come round the house to be heard a chaffinch calling at my window about a week he did not come when I put out some breadcrumbs. The are very busy eating the Thorn berries which are nearly all gone They have not attacked the Holly tree yet – I suppose the berries are not quite ripe enough, being still rather yellow. The leaves are falling very rapidly and suddenly from the trees, without changing colour as much as usual; it must be due to the sudden cold after an unusually long warm summer. Yesterday There was a good deal of wind, and the Plane tree at our back gate was shedding its leaves at a great rate. There had been a frost in the night, and one could hear the new leaves falling on the crisped old ones, a continual pattering sound like rain

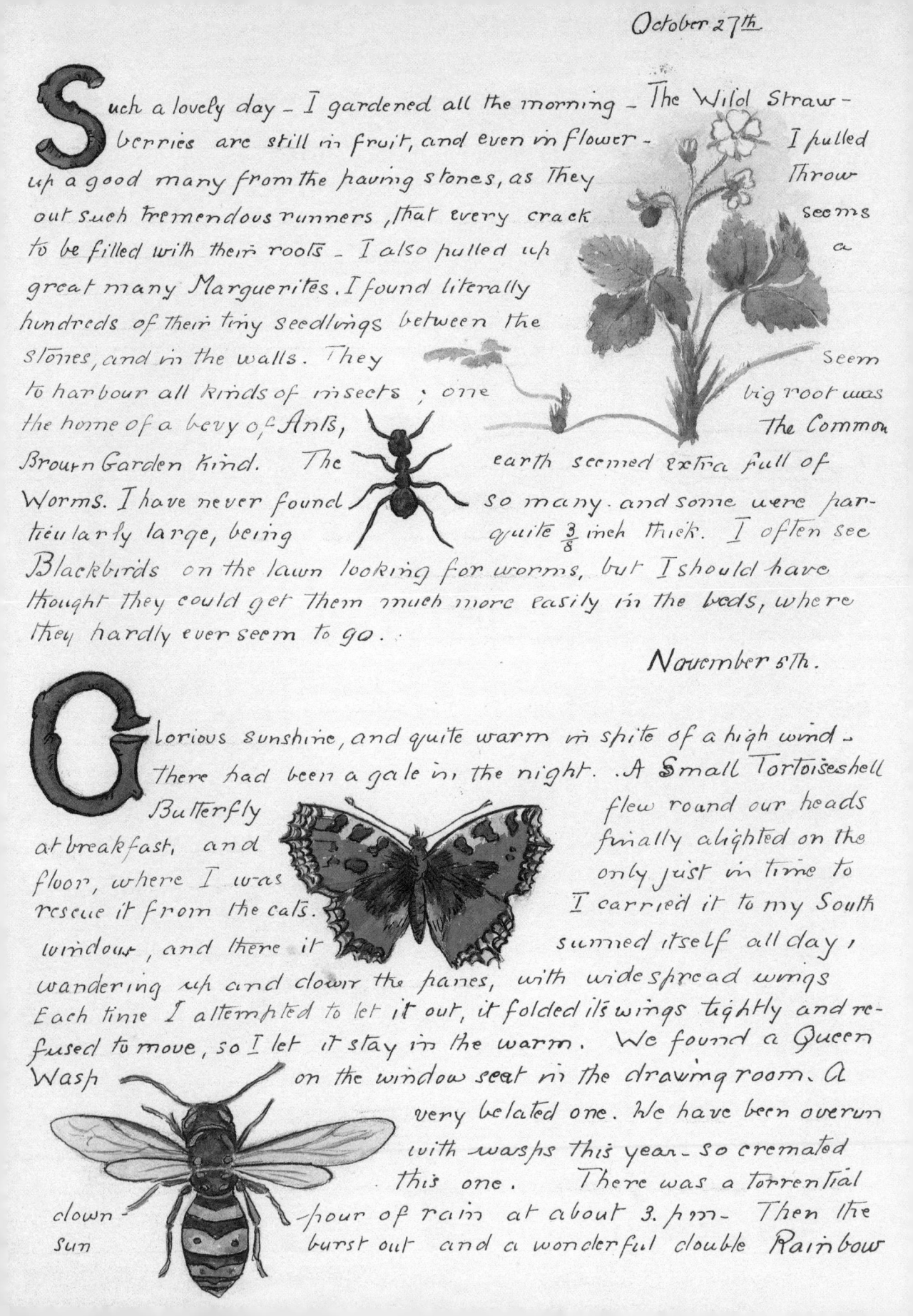

October 27th.

Such a lovely day – I gardened all the morning – The Wild Straw-berries are still in fruit, and even in flower – I pulled up a good many from the paving stones, as they throw out such tremendous runners, that every crack seems to be filled with their roots – I also pulled up a great many Marguerites. I found literally hundreds of their tiny seedlings between the stones, and in the walls. They seem to harbour all kinds of insects ; one big root was the home of a bevy of Ants, The Common Brown Garden kind. The earth seemed extra full of Worms. I have never found so many. and some were par-ticularly large, being quite $\frac{3}{8}$ inch thick. I often see Blackbirds on the lawn looking for worms, but I should have thought they could get them much more easily in the beds, where they hardly ever seem to go.

November 5th.

Glorious sunshine, and quite warm in spite of a high wind – There had been a gale in the night. A Small Tortoiseshell Butterfly flew round our heads at breakfast, and finally alighted on the floor, where I was only just in time to rescue it from the cats. I carried it to my South window, and there it sunned itself all day, wandering up and down the panes, with widespread wings Each time I attempted to let it out, it folded its wings tightly and re-fused to move, so I let it stay in the warm. We found a Queen Wasp on the window seat in the drawing room. A very belated one. We have been overrun with wasps this year – so cremated this one. There was a torrential down- hour of rain at about 3. pm – Then the sun burst out and a wonderful double Rainbow

appeared. I have never seen an entirely
perfect one before, and the colours
were intense, ranging from vivid
emerald green, to deep mauve.
From where I stood, it framed
the house, one end rising from
the hill to the West, and the
other losing itself in the
valley to the East. The rain soon ceased, and the evening was beautiful.

November 7th.

The morning was radiant, and it was quite hot in the sunshine. There was no wind; and evidently taking advantage of the fine weather the Tortoiseshell butterfly must have flown out of my East window for when I came in from the garden, he was gone. His place was soon taken by a Common Drone Fly, who had been buzzing about on my ceiling the night before. There seem to be a good many of these flies about the house. They are quite four times the size of an ordinary House Fly - with yellow and black bodies, more like a bee, but not hairy - and soft like the latter. And they make a great deal of noise knocking against things with their hard bodies as they fly about. There are hundreds of Blue Bottles on the ivy on the house, and they rise in buzzing swarms, every time one goes near them. The colouring of the Bluebottle is really lovely and one could admire it if one could only forget the repulsive things it feeds on.

November 18th

Owls have been very noisy at night lately, calling to each other on the hill and across the valley. A Robin came chirping at breakfast time, and we threw him some bread. It was pouring with rain. He chose a large piece out of a puddle, and carried it away to eat under the shelter of the little bush. He is the first to come to be fed this year. A few days ago a Robin tried to hang on to one of the cocoanuts, but found he could not manage it.

A **L**ovely sunny morning. Two birds came for crumbs, a Robin and a male chaffinch. By Christmas time there will be no berries on our holly tree, if the Blackbirds and Thrushes go on as they are doing now. If they ate all the berries one would not mind so much, but they are pecking off and throwing down, more than they eat – the ground is strewn with berries. The Blackbirds are worse than the Thrushes, one wonders why they come at all, as there are plenty of worms about, and the ground is quite soft as the weather has been so wet and mild.

A **B**lue-Tit came today, to one of the cocoanuts – I watched a Black-bird for a long time, eating holly berries, and saw him de-vour ten, he would have eaten more if another Blackbird had not come and chased him away. They swallow the berries one after another, whole – in rapid succession, and after each swallow, give a loud "chuck" either as a mark of appreciation, or an aid to digestion? The Blackbirds are very quarrelsome, and one hears continuous sounds of fighting and disturbance in the tree. It has been a very mild day, and there was a Bee in the drawing room, visiting all the flowers in turn.

A **W**onderfully fine and sunny day. It was so warm gardening in the morning, that I had to discard my coat. I planted new Tulip Bulbs all along the narrow beds at the foot of the walls – I laid all the bulbs on top, in position first, and when I came to put them in, I found on several, a tiny little glistening greeny black Beetle about $\frac{1}{16}$ inch long, with very fine antennae, they were winged, as directly I touched the bulbs, they flew away. I came upon an enormous brown and yellow toad, under the centre of a large mass of rock plant on the wall, near the foot, and in rather a damp corner. Moles are plentiful in the garden this autumn, there are little brown mounds of earth everywhere, and in some places great raised ridges across the grass, where they have tunneled from one bed to another. I picked quite a large bunch of "Cranfordia" yellow chrysanthemums, all in perfect condition— There should be about ten Goldfish in the Lily Pond, but only four seem to have survived, unless others appear later from under the Lily roots. One never sees the fish all through the summer as the Lily leaves entirely cover the pond.

November 28th

Yesterday morning I saw a Goldfinch in the plum tree at the back of the house. This is the very first I have seen round here, though our predecessor told us they used to build in the Rose Garden in the Yew hedge. Today the first of Bullfinches made his appearance in the Spirea tree, accompanied by his wife. They come every year, when all the leaves are gone, and eat the seeds which hang in brown bunches on the bare stems. Last year about three or four pair came every day till not a seed was left on the tree, then they all vanished. This is the only time of year we see them, and they never come near the house.

December 1st.

We have had several days of rain lately, and gardening has been difficult as the earth was so sodden. Today after a misty morning the sun shone, and I was able to put in some more bulbs. I found some quite pretty little snails, with golden yellow shells.. I wonder if they do as much harm as the large grey ones do. We have hundreds of the latter, they

live in large families in between the stones in the walls, and come
out at dusk and eat off the tulips at the base of the stalks,
and nibble large holes in the leaves.    There is not a single berry
left on our holly tree, the Blackbirds and Thrushes have eaten
them all, and are now busy hunting about among the rock plants
for those they threw down when there were still plenty on the Tree.

December 4th

I saw a lovely Cock Pheasant on the garden wall this morning  He has been over several times lately, and enjoys
pick- ing about in the freshly dug flower beds. Two years
ago a Hen Pheasant came to the Terrace
and ate crumbs with
the smaller birds under
the dining room window. but she only
came once. Some times about eight or nine come
in through the hedge, and walk in single file across
the lawn, and go up the bank, and disappear in the direction
of the marshy part of the field below the copse.

December 7th.

I Gathered a lovely bunch of hink Roses
in the bud, which came out
at once in water. There are a good
many more to come, if the frosts
do not touch them. The weather
has been quite mild lately with a
little rain at night.   Now that
the beds have been dug, there are very
few flowers left to pick for the
house Antirrhinums are still flowering
here and there on the bank. I cut them back
well after the first flowers were over and They
have thrown out. many new shoots.

December 8th.

A lovely day, followed by a most wonderful sunset. At 4o/c the whole sky was a mass of fleecy shrimp pink clouds, and everything was bathed in a glowing pink light. Later the night was very still and clear, and the stars shone brightly. On the 5th we had the loveliest sunrise I have ever seen in England. Blackdown was silhouetted against a sky of turquoise blue, streaked with vivid pink clouds edged with fiery gold, while above the deepest sky blue appeared between long feathery mauve and pink clouds. These wonderful colours lasted for than half an hour In spite of "A red sky in the morning, is the shepherds warning" we had a beautiful day.

December 16th.

We had the first really hard frost of the season last night, followed by a heavenly          day - The sun shone and the frost sparkled like                    tiny diamonds on leaves and grass. The birds were                    evidently feeling the cold, for they came                    for crumbs in a little flock at                    breakfast time. The Chaffinches were                    first upon the scene, then came the Robin,                    the Nuthatch, the Blackbird etc. The Bullfinches came back to the Spirea tree yesterday. After the 28th hou they did not reappear till the 15th inst. Now there are three pair hard at work on the seeds.
flowers in the garden. - A Campanula                    There are still a few
and a Primula Denticulata will soon be                    is doing its best to bloom
few small pieces of Stock and                    out. there are even a
                   Antirrhinum still left.

December 20th

Such a lovely day; it was quite hot gardening in the sun. I put in the last of my bulbs - Sir Watkin daffodils from last year — and did some weeding among the rock beds - The Couch grass spreads

terribly                    and there is a peculiar kind in the upper beds
which has         short thick   tufts of green blades on every shoot.
A Small       Tortoiseshell butterfly appeared in my South window, and         wandered up and down, spreading its         wings
in the warmth   A Blue bottle buzzed                noisily
about the                 room            trying
to make one think it was summer.                  One
poor S. Tortoiseshell butterfly I found          dead
on the hall floor.     A darling little Wren         disported
itself on the roof of the porch among the feathery      clematis
seeds, in search of insects.     The last two nights have been
brilliantly light - the full moon coming up pale gold, and setting
a delicate silver.

December 22<sup>nd</sup>

I Picked
yellow - today -             in spite of a very hard frost
during the             night.  Going round the
garden I             found a Double Blue
Primrose -             some pale pink Stock, and
several sprigs of Lithospermum         Heavenly Blue - which I picked and put in a tiny amber   vase.  It has been a bitterly cold
day, with a North Wind blowing - and it looks like snow coming.

about six more good roses, red and

December 23<sup>rd</sup>

Woke to find the ground white with a very fine thin layer of snow.
which melted away directly the sun was up. It was an icy
cold day with a keen wind blowing. The sun set in a sheet of pure
gold with a heavy bank of black clouds above it.

# 1927

**S**uch an exquisite day; the hint of Spring in it. Every-thing was bathed in glowing sunshine _ I found our first Snowdrop out on the bank. Most flowers seem to be later coming up this year than last; yet the winter has not really been at all severe. first with a real

January 27th.

**A**fter being confined to the house for a week, I found a great change in the garden. The rock part is bristling with tips of hyacinths, narcissi, tulips etc, and crocuses are up quite two inches and more _ There are quantities of Aconites, their buttercup yellow heads glistening above their Toby frills of bright green leaves. There are plenty of Christ-mas Roses, and in much better condition than usual as a rule they have nearly all been nibbled at by slugs. There are a few primroses in bloom, wild ones I transplanted, but I have seen none in the hedges so far.

February 15th.

**A H**eavy grey mist has been hanging over everything for over a week, with rare intervals of brilliant sunshine, when the fog lifted for a few hours. On the night of the 13th, the moon and stars shone brightly, and everything was clear _ but with the dawn the fog returned as thick as ever. An owl hooted loudly in the big chestnut tree across the road, and I looked out just in time to catch a glimpse of a large dark form, flapping noiselessly away to a tree further up the lane; there he sat and hooted again and again, but I could hear no response to his call, finally he flew away up the valley, the hoots growing fainter and fainter in the distance. It must have been a Brown Owl, by its cry "Tu-whit-tu whoo"

**A**s I was motoring up the lane about 3.30 pm I saw a weasel crossing the road, trailing after him a dead rat. At the sound of the car he dropped it, and darted across to the bank where he hid in a clump of brambles. I got out and looked at the rat, it seemed to have no wound of any kind, but the weasel is very neat in the way it kills, and merely makes a tiny hole in the jugular vein, and then draws the blood. – I crossed to the bramble bush and "froze", and in a moment the weasel popped out his head, and we mutually took a good look at each other! but he would not venture out till I had gone – directly I was back in the car, he emerged cautiously and collected his prey. The Weasel is not pretty in shape, being very long in the body, and short in the legs. and his tail goes into a point at the tip – "but he has quite a pretty little face with a long flat forehead, and wonderfully bright eyes. His colouring is red-brown, paler under the body. unlike the Stoat, he does not change his coat in winter. He lives among rocks and stones, and is very useful as a scavenger. He also keeps down the rabbits, and usually makes his home near a rabbit warren.

March. 1st.

**The L**ast days of February were terribly wet and stormy, but today was quite mild and fine. The yellow Crocus are in full bloom, those under the dining-room window are a serried mass of gold in the sunshine. Scillas are out, and hyacinth buds are showing their colour. Aubretia and single arabis are beginning to flower, and tulip leaves are well up. Nearly all the Crocus under the pergola have been eaten by mice.

March 2.nd

**A G**lorious spring day, with warm sunshine. On our way to Guildford we saw some lovely "Palm" or "Pussy-Willow" in the hedges. I think they were Goat-Willow, as they were bushy trees with short stems, throwing

March 3rd

**R**eally lovely day, warm about noon, but getting chilly towards evening
The crocus opened wide to the sun, and Humble Bees were
very busy among them, gathering honey _ They made such a summer
-y sound. Frogs spawned about two days ago, in the pond outside, and in
the upper and lower ponds in the garden. Other years they have only spawned
in the centre pond. The spawn is a jelly substance looking like
masses of transparent boiled tapioca with a black speck in each
swollen grain. There are a few Primroses, very short in the wood, but
none in the hedges so far.

March 11th

**L**ooking out of my East window at 6.10 AM _ I saw a large Rabbit dashing
up the lane. Arrived behind the old chest-
nut stump he "froze" _ and in a minute or two I
saw our black cat Nicco emerging from the
wood, and sheltering behind the Bramble bushes _ he cautiously peered round
down the lane, in the direction from which the rabbit had come _ The latter
moved not a muscle till Nicco had come out from his hiding place, and had
disappeared into the hedge _ then he bolted across to the safe shelter of the
wood_

March 12th

**T**his morning at 6 o/c I saw four rabbits
feeding by the old chestnut tree _ it is a
place with them, and they come nearly
morning now.

favorite
every

March 13.

**E**xamined the frog spawn in the ponds. There is no sign of life
I yet_ but the spots are developing into semicircles
I picked some Primroses, my first this year, in the
wood opposite. Masses of bluebell leaves are up, but there
are no signs of buds yet_

# Elham Kent

Such a heavenly day. There is a marsh here quite close to the house, and quantities of Moorhens. They run about the meadows, and swim in the fascinating little streams made by the "February Filldyke" rains. They are very tame, and come quite close to the house. One hears their strange harsh cry at dusk.

March 17th.

Another glorious day, but with rather a cold wind. There was a frost in the night — We were able to sit out in the garden in the sun, for more than an hour in the afternoon. The Frog spawn here is quite different to that at Fernhurst, being far less Transparent — It is dirty in colour, in spite of the water being very clear, and the jelly instead of being very soft is in distinct little round balls, made up in cone shaped blocks, going to a point under the water. We found a good many frogs in the well — some dead, some dying; they evidently come in from the field, through the over-flow pipe. It is most amusing watching the Starlings here. In the evening They collect in huge companies by the thousand in the tall Elm Trees in the next field Their screaming and chattering is quite distracting, every now and then They all rise in a great black cloud circle round and round the tree, after finally settling there to roost. Then suddenly the babel of sound, there is a silence, and all is peaceful once more. The Starling lives on worms, insects and beetles, and one often sees them perched on the backs of sheep, insect hunting

We found a centipede ~~~~~~~~~~~~~~~~~~~~ on the landing window sill. It was about two and a half inches long, when it stretched itself to its full length, and when it contracted itself it became about half its length. Its body was scaley, and its legs innumerable.

This is a great Sheep farming district. and it is lambing time. No dogs are allowed out without owners, for fear they should worry the sheep. and if they are seen alone they are shot. Every field is full of sheep. I see them from my window every morning being fed. by two men who bring sacks of food, and scatter it along the ground. The sheep come running from every corner, with a great deal of baaing. later in the day a cart load of mangles is brought for them. The baby lambs are very sweet. and very shaky on their long legs. some of them are very frisky and play like puppies. Nearly every sheep has two young ones.

In the evening after dark we found a frog, or Toad, carrying a young one on its back. The baby was having a regular "piggy-back" ride. it looked quite large enough to be on its own. We were not sure whether it was a Toad or a Frog, as having a little one on its back, it probably could not jump as a frog generally does. as far as we could see by lamp light, it was yellowish in colour. with dark spots all over it. Earlier in the evening we had found a frog hopping about in the hall.

A Song Thrush sings every evening in an apple tree in the orchard. He sits there for a long time, and sings a most wonder- full song, as if his heart was bursting with happiness. He is smaller than the Missel Thrush, and darker in colour, altogether a more re- fined looking bird. There is a Thrushes nest in the hedge, a last years one - most beautifully made, with twigs, and lined with mud. I have not found any of this years nests yet - perhaps the branches are too bare to afford any privacy. The Fan tailed Pigeons we brought down on the 16th, and wired in to a new cote, began to make a nest this morning - We gave them a bunch of hay and straw - and they are most am- using to watch the husband selects the pieces and passes them through the doorway one at a time to his wife, who arranges them inside the cote - from time to time the husband goes in to see what kind of a job she is making of it.

March 22nd.

A Grey day, and drizzling. I saw a Blackbird having a very thorough bath in the water filled holes, made by the cows hoofs at the edge of the pond and a Pied Wagtail was running about the margin, picking up insects. At Folkestone Almond blossom was lovely.

Fernhurst.

As soon as I got home I went up to see the frogspawn. All the jelly has dissolved and there are dense masses of tiny wriggling black tadpoles - The garden has come on wonderfully in the week I have been away. Hyacinths are in full bloom, also Narcissii, Scillas, single white and pink Arabis and Hepaticas. The crocus are beginning to go over. Aubretia in all shades is colouring rapidly, and a few kinds are fully out in glowing masses. Grape Hyacinths are almost in bloom, and daffodils are out in the grass, also Periwinkles. All plants are beginning to shoot, and trees are in full bud.

March 23rd

There was a tremendous storm in the night. On our way to Guildford we saw masses of Almond in full bloom   also Wild Plum, and Blackthorn- I staked up all the   hyacinths in the evening - as the nights storm had   laid them low.

March 24th

Had a birds shelter   put up in the orchard- in view of the drawing   room windows. — and had the box nest on   the pergola moved further down the pillar, as the cats   could reach it from above.

March 25th

A Day of rain and hail storms. Found two dead rats in the garden evidently killed by the cats.

March 26th

Saw a pair of Blackbirds inspecting the Box nest   on The pergola. Mrs B hung on the edge of the hole   and finally went in, while Mr B sat on top. I don't think they   found the house suitable as they both flew away and did not return.   There are masses   of primroses in the woods, also Lent Lillies, (or tiny   Daffodils) — White Violets   are out on our walls, and   in the grass on   the green, and all along   the foot   of our outer wall.

I found my first Anemone in the woods. In the evening
there was rain and hail and then appeared
a wonderful vivid double Rainbow,
which lasted for about fifteen minutes.

March 27th. '27

I Found Lesser Celandines in the hedge in the lane, and the
Pied Wagtails appeared here for
the first time this
year. I think a pair must
be building in the ivy on the house,
they strut up and down on the top of the wall below, and
run round the stone rim of the Lily pond catching flies.
Blue Tits and Nuthatches have been to the porch nest box,
but the cats get at them, and we cannot keep them off, they manage to
climb or jump up, in spite of wire netting on the porch side. Anemone
Pulsatilla is in flower.

March 28th.

A lovely day, it was so warm in the sun, that we were
able to sit and sew out of doors. I found
the first Cowslips → in bloom in our field.
and many Celandines among
the marshy parts. Nuthatches
are very busy in the box nest in the porch
one hears a constant sound of tapping within.
We never see more than one bird at a time at the nest.

March 31st.

A Radiant morning — we motored to London early. All Nature
was putting on its delicate green mantle of Spring, and
the Parks were gay with daffodils.

A Showery day. I found a large Toad under a big clump of forgetmenots which I was digging up. He was very indignant at being disturbed and lumbered away into a crevise in the wall. He has a nice damp place near the well. The Toad has much shorter legs than the Frog. and crawls instead of leaping. His body is coarse and clumsy and encrusted with lumps. He has no teeth, and lives on slugs and insects.

Tadpoles are still in black wriggling masses in the ponds, and the water above them is covered with frothy white bubbles. The Nuthatch is very busy at the porch nest, cementing round the edge of the opening to make it smaller. Every few minutes he brings a large lump of mud in his beak, plasters it on, and moulds it into shape with his beak, with much tapping. I cannot take the lid off the box to see the nest, as the nuthatches always cement it all round the crack, to keep the draught out.

After three days from home I went up to inspect the tadpoles, and not one was to be seen. I cannot think what has become of them There are a good many Newts, but no sign of those thousands of tadpoles. On the 5th they had no legs, so I do not think they can already have turned into frogs. The Nuthatches have finished cementing the nest. and I think Mrs N must be sitting. A pair of Blackbirds have a nest in the ivy on the wall under my window.

Summer time began. It was almost a relief as lately the birds have been so noisy in the early morning, waking me at about 4.45, with their song and chatter. A Missel Thrush sits in the top branches of a tall tree outside my East window, and sings for literally hours on end. He must have a nest near by - He has a large variety of notes, but is very insistent on some of them - Our Camelias are in bloom, and the bushes are a mass of buds.

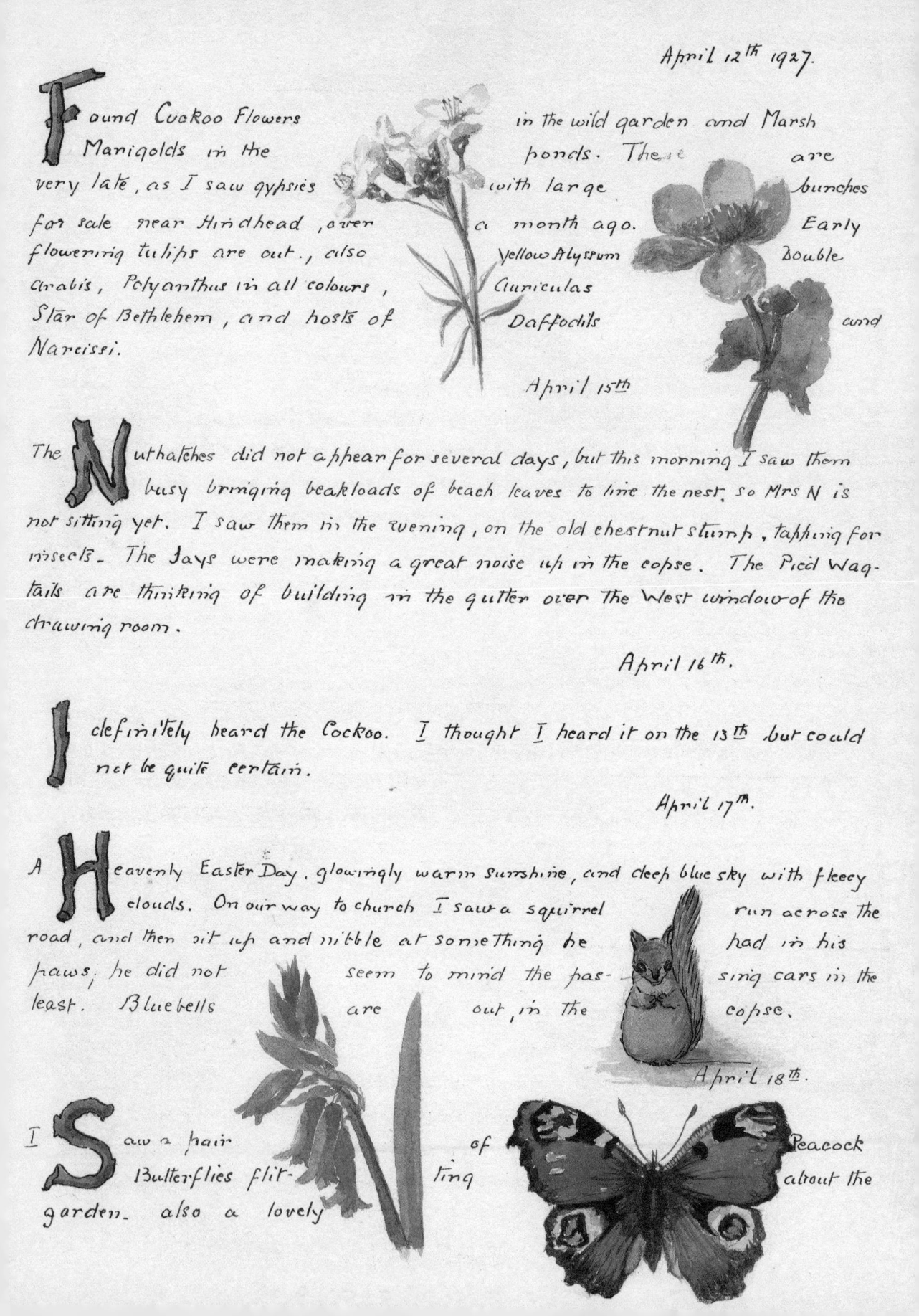

April 12th 1927.

Found Cuckoo Flowers Marigolds in the very late, as I saw gypsies for sale near Hindhead, over flowering tulips are out., also Arabis, Polyanthus in all colours, Star of Bethlehem, and hosts of Narcissi.

in the wild garden and Marsh ponds. These with large a month ago. Yellow Alyssum Auriculas Daffodils

are bunches Early Double

and

April 15th

The Nuthatches did not appear for several days, but this morning I saw them busy bringing beakloads of beach leaves to line the nest, so Mrs N is not sitting yet. I saw them in the evening, on the old chestnut stump, tapping for insects. The Jays were making a great noise up in the copse. The Pied Wagtails are thinking of building in the gutter over the West window of the drawing room.

April 16th.

I definitely heard the Cuckoo. I thought I heard it on the 13th but could not be quite certain.

April 17th.

A Heavenly Easter Day. glowingly warm sunshine, and deep blue sky with fleecy clouds. On our way to church I saw a squirrel run across the road, and then sit up and nibble at something he had in his paws; he did not seem to mind the passing cars in the least. Bluebells are out, in the copse.

April 18th.

I Saw a pair of Peacock Butterflies flitting about the garden. also a lovely

Brimstone Butterfly.                                    The field below the
copse is carpeted with                                  Dog Violets.
I also found Wood Sorrel                                and
Ground Ivy. I got a step                                ladder
and looked into the Black                               bird's nest
with some difficulty, there are fledglings in it about four or five days
old.

April 21st.

I saw a Ladybird                    wandering over my tablecloth when I was having
    tea at Waterloo                 Station. I suppose it must have come in on a
    bunch of flowers.               It had two spots. The two principal kinds of
Ladybird are                        the "Two-spotted" and the "Seven Spotted". I
had one of the former on my window about a fortnight ago. The Ladybird
is a most useful insect as it lives on the plant-lice, that blight roses and hops.
When attacked it throws out an unpleasantly scented fluid - its only means
of protection —

April 22nd

Lilac flowers are in full bud. I watched the Pond          Skaters on the
    lily pond. They have three pairs of legs, the          first pair
    just below the head the second at the lower end of the chest. These
are their oars. the last pair act entirely as rudders and are never used
for swimming — Pond skaters live on dead and living insects —

April 25th

I Saw a Queen Wasp on the ivy outside my East window at 6. AM. The
    weather for the last fortnight has been wonderful, not a drop of rain
until today when there was a slight drizzle in the early morning. The ground
is getting very dry and hard, and many plants in the garden are beginning
to shrivel.

April 26th.

Young Blackbirds have not left the nest yet. I found several nests in
    the field — two Blackbirds - which are always rather clumsy and
untidy looking — one tiny one, too high up to see., and one which I think
is a Chaffinches, made of bright green moss, and welded onto the fork of a small May

free, in full view of all passers by; there were two eggs in the nest, which is beautifully lined with hair and feathers.

April 27th 1927.

There was a great deal of noise in the Blackbirds nest in the early morning. I found two Blackbirds nests, with the hens sitting, in the thickets in the lane, rather to high up to see well. Saw Herb Robert for the first time this year the lower leaves just beginning to turn red, also the stalks, with are covered with the finest silver hairs. The plant has a curious aromatic scent. Greater Stitchwort is in full bloom in the hedges. It has five petals, so deeply indented that it appears to have ten. The five sepals are very pointed, and are edged with silvery white, five stamens are short and five long. The stems are square and brittle, and the leaves long and pointed, like grass, springing in joined pairs from the stalk. I also found Common Bugle in the lane, It has a wonderful purpleish square stem, with many petals in pairs, set on alternate sides. The flowers grow in circles round the stem where the leaves join it.

April 28th

Early in the morning I saw Mrs Blackbird taking worms to her babies In the evening I touched the nest gently, and there was a wild clamour of voices, and necks and mouths stretched up over the edge. I went to see the doubtful nest in the field and found three eggs, but no bird — later I came back from the opposite direction, and creeping up very cautiously I caught the bird sitting before she saw me. — it was a chaffinch. I found quite a large patch of Early Purple Orchis growing under the bushes at the side of a field.

April 29th.

It rained in the night, and on into the morning, and everything looked so refreshed. but there was not sufficient to soak far into the ground — and after a afternoon and evening everything looked quite parched brilliant I cannot think when the young Blackbirds are going again to leave the nest — They must be at least thirteen days old, and are fully feathered. They were asleep when I looked into the nest at 6. pm —

April 30th.

I fed the little Blackbirds in the nest with worms at 10.AM. there was no sign of the parents anywhere - When I left the house at 2 pm I found the two babies on the ground under the nest all alone. I put them back, but they instantly hopped out into the branches. E.B.L. found them on the ground later, and put them back again. When we came in 7.30 pm they had finally disappeared. I only hope the parents got them safely away from the cats.

May 1st.

Went down to the field and found the Chaffinch sitting tight on her nest. At Marley when I went out to tea, I saw a poor little Robin which had lost its entire beak. it looked as if it had been broken off in a trap. it came for food to the house - it could not eat anything hard, but seemed to manage soft crumbs - it looked quite fat and well except for the beak, and was extraordinarily tame. Our Wistaria is just beginning to bloom., luckily it has not been touched by the late frosts we are still having.

May 2nd.

I found a Chaffinche's nest in the Yew hedge, the young birds had just flown and were cheeping about in the bushes. I also found a Blackbirds nest near by, with young about four days old. There is a wonderful little mossy nest hanging out near the end of a thin bough of the Yew tree. E.B.L. thinks it is a Golden Crested Wren's, but I have never seen any about. The nest is unfinished as yet.

May 4th.

A very hot, close day, with heavy clouds, but still no rain.

May 5th.

I saw a Cuckoo being attacked by two small birds, on the topmost branch of a distant tree; the Cuckoo finally flew away still pursued by one of the small birds. I wonder if they were trying to prevent her from laying an egg in their nest. In the evening I saw a Flycatcher on the bird shelter; the first I have seen this year. We had rain. but not enough to really soak the ground thoroughly-

May 8th 1927.

I found buttercups in the wild garden. on some rock plants. The baby — Some of the Rock Roses Linum Flavum. The Laburnum On our way to London I saw White May. and Laburnum in full White Chestnut. As we passed over a Wild Duck flew overhead. and a Seven Spot Ladybird Blackbirds are well feather- are in bloom, and also is covered with blossom. masses of Pink and bloom, also Pink and Hammersmith Bridge

May 9th.

From the train, London to Folkestone, I noticed quantities of Purple Flag Iris in the gardens, and a wonderful Golden field of Mustard. Pink Campion were in bloom along the line, and the Hop crops were about one foot high. in France I saw Water Avens on many of the ponds we passed.

May 10th

Italy.

We passed a field of green corn with scarlet Poppies- and acres of what looked like blue Veronica. Nasturtiums were in full bloom at one station, and at Rahallo I saw Oranges growing on the trees — the trees in many cases have both flowers and fruit at the same time. Side by side with the oranges, were masses of roses, red and yellow, and Eucalyptus in flower. I saw both White and yellow wild Iris — Wild roses, and Pink Mallow. In one place the hay had been cut. We passed miles of Vines, grown in many different ways; the prettiest are on pergolas, about 7 feet high. when these are parralel and close together, the Vines look like lovely fresh green carpets spread in mid air. Others are stretched like ropes between two small poplar trees — or cut short and tied to small stakes. these are rather untidy looking.

In Florence. May 15th.

I watched the Pigeons on the Church opposite our hotel — There are small square holes ☐ all over ☐ the walls ☐ and in each hole is a pigeons nest, well out of reach of every one. At Fiesole I heard a very familiar song, and looking up saw two poor little Chaffinches in a tiny cage in a window. — In the gardens There are lovely borders of Pale Mauve Iris, and dwarf pink Monthly Roses. There are quantities of Ilex Trees – Palms etc.

May 22nd

The wild Roses are simply lovely; they grow in small bushes, with very long sprays covered with blossoms. I saw an extraordinary great black flying Beetle at Feltre but could not quite see if it had 2 wings or four. two I think. Hair bells, or rather Cam-panulas, grow in profu-sion in the crevices in the rocks. I found ripe wild Strawberries, and Saponaria. also Vetch.

May 23rd.

I Saw Meadow Sweet in the fields, and quantities of Valerian on the mountain sides, near Lake Garda. I saw Sand Martins in the sandy cliffs.

May 30th.

Fernhurst. England.

When I came home after three weeks abroad I found everything very changed in the garden. all the Tulips over, also Aubretia, Arabis & Oriental Poppies are in bloom; Rock Roses, Lithospermum, Saponaria, Catmint Lupins, Cerastium, Linum, Perenne. and Flavum. Mrs Sinkin Pinks. Frankia. Geums, and a few Roses. I hear the Blackbirds flew on the 14th.

May 31st.

I Saw the Nuthatches taking tiny smooth green caterpillars to the Porch Nest. and feeding The clamourous little mouths — The parents are enlarging the entrance hole. In the evening I saved a baby Rabbit from Martie. and took it down The lane and put it into the wood. It was terrified, but not hurt.

June 1st 1927.

While I was gardening I watched the Nuthatches feeding their young. When Mr N saw me looking, he gave a loud warning "T3–T3" and the babies instantly ceased twittering, and subsided into the nest. Later I went quite close up, and the babies kept putting their heads out in turn, and peered upwards and downwards, they seemed as if they were coming out every moment, and their heads were fully feathered. A Baby Blackbird kept hopping about near me as I was planting geraniums. he was very tame, and came within three feet of me.

June 2nd

Looked out early, but saw no sign of the Nuthatches moving. Then at 8.0½ there was a flutter at my window, and there was a tiny Nuthatch sitting in my open window. It had a good look in, and then at a call from one of the parents away it went. I flew downstairs and was just in time to see the last two leaving the branches round the nest. They all gathered on the old chestnut tree, and the air was full of the sound of their T3 T3 T3 as they flew about. Towards the end of the day they all disappeared. — I picked some lovely Roses and Nelly Moser Clematis. I killed a Hornet in the drawingroom.

June 3rd

Yesterday two Wrens were making a great noise in a tree near the summer house. and Whitethroats near the ponds. This morning I went to look for their nests. and found the Wrens' suspended from the centre of the Summer House ceiling, — while I sat there quite quiet the wren came in with food, through a hole at the corner of the thatching. I could hear no sound from the babies. The nest is very untidy looking made of coarse dead grass. but it is wonderfully suspended, against a rafter. The Whitethroats' nest I found in the thorn bushes near the pond, about three feet from the ground, with four babies in it. I think they must be ready to fly. for when they saw me, two of them hopped out of the nest and disappeared into the bushes. It was quite impossible to collect them again so I hope the parents found them again all right. I had seen the nest before the eggs were laid, it is made of dried grass. horse hair and pieces of fluffy seed from the bullrushes near by.

June 4th

I found a tiny rabbit in the wood. it must have got pinched in the gate as I opened it. it cried terribly, and could not walk, yet it seemed uninjured. I tried putting it into a burrow. but it just sat hunched up. so I took it to the kitchen - and later it completely recovered, and was carried back to the wood, where it ran down a burrow. I also found a baby Missel Thrush on the path - It opened it's mouth to be fed. but when I went to pick it up, it hopped away into a thicket. It was not quite old enough to fly. but there was no sign of nest or parents anywhere - There are quantities of Yellow Water Iris in the marshy part of the field, and I found Spotted Orchis by the pond. also Hop Trefoil, and creeping Cinquefoil.

June 10th

I Saw a Squirrel crossing the road at the top of Fridays Hill.

June 11th

There are a good many young Jay's about. and one came and sat in the holly tree at breakfast time. I found the bottom of a wrens nest under the laurels. it must have been pulled down by the cats. It was lined with feathers and had several cracked eggs sticking to it.

June 12th

Spotted flycatcher and it's baby came and sat on my East window sill, and later the baby sat on the telephone wire outside for a long time; and looked in.

June 13th

Watched a father Chaffinch feeding it's hen baby on crumbs on the ter- race. such a large baby, it looked quite big enough to feed itself, but the father had to keep pushing the crumbs down it's throat.

June 15th 1927.

**S**aw quantities of wild Roses along the line as I went up to town.

(Dog)

June 17th

**T**he weather broke, and it rained all the morning - the garden needed the rain very badly.

June 18th.

**I** found a lovely big brown Frog in the field - pale coffee coloured back. With dark brown patches at each side of the face, greenish yellow under body. There was a gale in the evening, and torrents of rain.

June 19th

**W**atched a hen Chaffinch feeding its baby. - a cock chaffinch often brings its baby to the bird shelter, and the holly tree to feed. The Wrens sing every day outside my east window, and the dining room. Honeysuckle is in full bloom.

June 23rd

**H**osts of birds feed on the shelter, in spite of the fact that the earth is quite soft after the rain. A cock chaffinch brings two young, who stand in front of him and clamour to be fed, wagging their heads from side to side, their mouths gaping wide.

June 24th

**C**haffinches especially the young ones, are very tame, and feed at the open drawing room window, within a few inches of us, while we stand there talking - I am trying to get them to eat out of my hand.

June 25th

**F**ound a dead Squirrel in our wood. I feel sure one of our cats had just killed it, for it was still limp and warm, it had a wound in the side of its neck. . I also found a tiny rabbit, dead, in the orchard.

Several Jays were making a terrible noise in the orchard, I found them busy in the plum-trees, and scared them off. They flew away screaming to the copse. From 5 to 6.30 is the time when there are most birds on the Shelter. Today there were baby Blue Tits, and Great Tits. Young Nuthatches Robins, Blackbirds, and Chaf- finches with their babies. The Blackbirds are very tiresome as they eat up the fat so quickly, and frighten the small birds away.

June 27<sup>th</sup>

I saw a Meadow-Brown Butterfly in the garden - a female. which has a large black spot with a little white one in the centre, on each front wing, instead of a dark spot with a white ring round, as the male has. It was such a cold day that we had a fire in the drawing room.

June 28<sup>th</sup>.

Saw a House Martin's nest under the eaves of a house in the village. The birds were flying low over the ground round about. Unlike the Swallow, their tails though forked are very short. and they have a broad white band round the body at the base of the tail.

June 29<sup>th</sup>

Got up at 5:50 to see the Eclipse of the Sun - and saw only an im- penetrable white mist, enveloping everything, and heard the drip drip of the falling rain. At 6.10 the mist cleared right away suddenly: then it grew darker. but never really dark. It was darkest at 6.15 when there was a curious yellow light over everything, rather like a London fog. At 6.20 it was quite light again - The eclipse had a depressing effect on the birds They hushed their song and sat in groups in the trees, probably wondering why roosting time had come again so soon! Later in the day it poured with rain. I have never seen so many birds on the shelter - Crowds of Chaffinches- one was very belligerent, and for quite ten minutes kept all other birds at bay, while he satisfied his hunger with the new crumbs I had

just thrown out. There were three and four Great Tits on the
cocoa-nut at the same time, all young ones. — The
Chaffinches are now so tame They come inside the drawingroom, window, and eat on the inner sill.

June 30th 1927.

At 11pm three curious flying beetles? appeared round the reading lamp
in my room. I cannot imagine what they were. rather like male
Glowworms, but I do not think They could be that. — Saw
dozens of Moorhen swimming about in Frensham Ponds.

July 1st.

The wettest day of the year — woke to pouring rain. and it only left off for
about an hour in the afternoon

July 2nd

On the way home from Bognor I saw a Yellow Hammer
or "Yellow Bunting" in a hedge. We have none
round here, and it is a very noticeable bird, with its bright
yellow head and breast. Many of the fields were scarlet
with poppies. I saw several flights of Swallows.

July 3rd

I saw a Grizzled Skipper Butterfly., rather an insignificant
little Thing, dark brown spotted with white.
and with wings family outlined with white. I found
Black Knapweed. a thistle-like flower with no prickles — also
White wild Roses. These are very sweetly scented, and
smaller than the pink variety, with creamy petals and
yellow centres. Two chaffinches came inside the window,
and fed for quite a long time

July 4th

Potentilla Miss Willmot is in flower in the garden. At tea the window
was shut, and we suddenly noticed a row of three chaffinch heads

peering in, They were waiting to come in for crumbs. A Blue Tit ventured on to the sill. but could not make up its mind to come in. They are very timid

July 6th 1927.

Evening Primroses are in bloom in the Garden.

July 7th

I saw quantities of Great Bindweed in the hedges on our way to Arundel. At Lilllehampton I saw Starlings on the hotel lawn. They are rather dishevelled un- finished looking birds- and make a great deal of noise.

July 11th.

Buddleia is just coming into bloom. Round Oxford I saw Vetch growing in great masses right to the top of the hedges. I also saw a great deal of Musk Mallow it has beautiful Rose coloured flowers. The air was fragrant with Meadow Sweet- Parsley was in full bloom, and the hedgerows thick with it. Here _ at Much Wenlock, from my bedroom window I see a Pied Wagtail going in to its nest- under the top of a roof oppo- site, and there are House Sparrow's nests behind the hotel name board on the wall. There were very heavy thunder showers in the evening, and it was quite dark at 7.30.

July 12th

Saw the Swallows at Their nests under the eaves at back of the hotel. They looked very dejected in the pouring rain. (Much-Wenlock)

July 13th

At Stranraer I watched the Sea-birds in the harbour _ and saw three Kinds. There were hundreds Congregated all over the sandy

flaß. The Brown Headed Gull — which I saw
following the plough about ten miles inland. This
Gull has a very dark brown heads and is frequently
called "Black Headed" - red bill and legs. —
The Common White while, bill
and legs yellow - the back and wings grey. black at the tips
with white points. I noticed young ones of this
Species, which have a mottled brown appearance.
The third kind was I think a Common Tern. the
top of the head and back of neck black. Back
and wings ash grey, Tail long and
forked. It flies quite differently to
the other Gulls. going from side to side, and
rising and falling frequently. I watched one for a long time, and it
kept darting right down into the water perpendicularly. evidently looking
for small fish. It made quite a splash each time, but I never saw it catch
anything.

July 14th 1927.

As we left Stranraer, all along Loch Ryan there were masses of Thrift
(Armeria) — I found Rest Harrow, Mauve Yarrow, Thyme
and quantities of Birds Foot Trefoil — I came
upon a Sky Lark which had just found some insect
by the Sea in the grass. On a rock a good
way out in the water I saw four Cormorants
in a row, and quite near the shore
one was seated all by himself
very up- right, his wings spread
to their utmost extent to dry. he had evidently been diving for fish. He looked
exact- ly like a "spread eagle" The
Cor- morant is not a graceful bird. it has a long hooked
beak, and clumsy body. it flies very rapidly in a
straight line - its long neck outstretched _ I think I saw
Jack Daws in a field _ two of them _ They were
like small Rooks, but with the back of the head and
neck grey, and they seemed a much greyer black all over.

July 15th.

"Jackdaw."

**I**mpressions of the day's run from **A**berfoyle to
Blue sky with fleecy clouds — Fields of young green
of Buttercups and Oxeye Daisies, bushes of Dog Roses — deep
and white. Glades of overhanging, interlacing Trees —
Lochs with wonderful reflections — water lillies. Green
with sheets of foxgloves. masses of yellow broom.
Flocks of Brown headed Gulls in the ploughed fields. Wild
tains, barren rocks, sullen skies with angry clouds. Mountain streams
falling over stoney beds. Fertile valleys and woods.

"**B**allater".
wheat.
pink
still
slopes
Heather.
lonely moun-

July 16th

**T**he gardens up here are about two months behind our Southern ones.
Pink May is still in bloom, Lupins and Oriental Poppies, which have long
been over with us. — also the Common mauve Rhododendrons.
"**I**mpressions of the day's run from Ballater to **A**rdgay."
Glorious deep blue sky, with billowy white clouds casting great shadows over
sunlit hills carpeted with carmine purple bell heather — hundreds of
scuttling rabbits. Masses of golden Broom. Deep blue of Moray Firth,
with blue mountains beyond.
We came suddenly on a Grouse                with her family of about
seven tiny babies. Three were sep-                arated from her, and
before we could pull up we had                passed right over the
top of them, leaving them safe, but                doubtless very bewilder-
ed in the middle of the road. We had                seen two other grouse
before, and they had hardly moved for                the car. I also saw
a large flock of                Peewits, (or Green Plovers) and many Brownheaded
Gulls, which seem                to be quite inland birds in Scotland. I found
yellow Rock Roses                Meadow's Crane's Bill — and Heartsease.

July 17th.

**F**rom **A**rdgay to **T**ongue. — The rabbits and Gulls up here are
every tame. At                Lairg the rabbits were running about between
the houses. and at                Tongue the Gulls sat about in the gardens. I had
one just outside my window. I saw an old Tramp, throw some pieces of bread

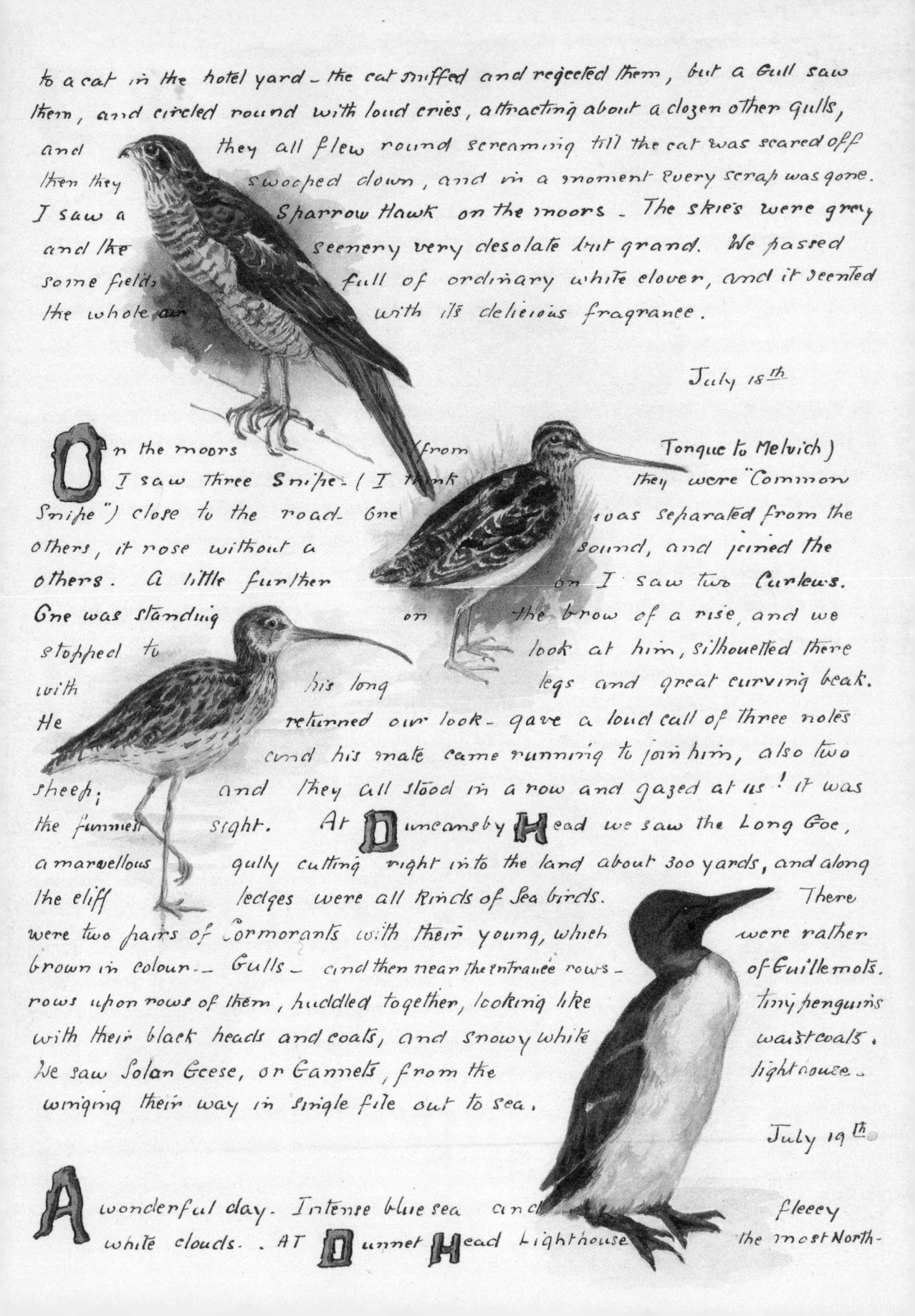

to a cat in the hotel yard — the cat sniffed and rejected them, but a Gull saw them, and circled round with loud cries, attracting about a dozen other Gulls, and they all flew round screaming till the cat was scared off then they swooped down, and in a moment every scrap was gone. I saw a Sparrow Hawk on the moors — The skies were grey and the scenery very desolate but grand. We passed some fields full of ordinary white clover, and it scented the whole air with its delicious fragrance.

July 18th

On the moors (from Tongue to Melvich) I saw three Snipe — (I think they were "Common Snipe") close to the road. One was separated from the others, it rose without a sound, and joined the others. A little further on I saw two Curlews. One was standing on the brow of a rise, and we stopped to look at him, silhouetted there with his long legs and great curving beak. He returned our look — gave a loud call of three notes and his mate came running to join him, also two sheep; and they all stood in a row and gazed at us! it was the funniest sight. At Duncansby Head we saw the Long Goe, a marvellous gully cutting right into the land about 300 yards, and along the cliff ledges were all kinds of Sea birds. There were two pairs of Cormorants with their young, which were rather brown in colour — Gulls — and then near the entrance rows — of Guillemots. rows upon rows of them, huddled together, looking like tiny penguins with their black heads and coats, and snowy white waistcoats. We saw Solan Geese, or Gannets, from the lighthouse — winging their way in single file out to sea.

July 19th

A wonderful day. Intense blue sea and fleecy white clouds. . AT Dunnet Head Lighthouse the most North-

erly point of Scotland we were lucky to meet a very intelligent lighthouse
keeper who was a bird lover - he knew all about sea birds, their nests and habits. We
stood on the cliffs and looked right down into the sea, where there
were hundreds of birds, strings of young Guillemots
swimming about in the water looking, from the height, like
cork floats on a net! Gannets→ were diving for fish, and I
saw a Lesser Black Backed Gull, the Lighthouse man told
us they are regular thieves, and go round turning
other birds off their eggs. As a rule the eggs
never fall off the ledges they are
laid on, being shaped so that they
only revolve but never roll. but he
has seen the sitting bird pull the egg off,
the rock with her when attacked by the Black Backed Gull.

He also showed us the Fulmar Petrel and told us that up
till now they have not nested on the North→ coast. but that this
year he has found twenty eight pairs nesting. They are
something like the Common Gull in body, but have a
larger hooked beak.   He pointed out a Razor
Bill and a Puffin, but they were too far off
to distinguish them properly.     Between
Melvich and Helmsdale we saw many "Highland Cattle"
red-brown with wide horns and long shaggy forelock -
the young ones were very sweet. I saw more Plovers
and a great Hooded Crow. This is larger than
the Carrion Crow. and instead of being
black all over, has a grey brown body.
It flies slowly and rather heavily.
I saw the first live Hare have ever seen - it was
feeding on the moor quite close to the road. The Hare is very like
the rabbit except that it is bigger in size
and has much longer longer back legs, which makes
it a much swifter runner.

July 20th

From Dornoch to Birnam. — Such a contrast to the brilliant sunshine of
yesterday. everything was grey and sad looking, the sea a dull green. the

mountains veiled in thick mist, at times the rain came down steadily, then the clouds broke and it cleared for a little. A Heron flew high over the road in front of us, its long legs outstretched behind it, and soared away over a wood. I noticed that though we passed many fields carpeted with white Clover, no fragrance reached us, as it does when the hot sun has been shining on it. I saw a Snipe walking across the road. Sheep are everywhere, on every mountain side, and in every field, and often lying in the middle of the road, they do not mind cars in the least, and move out of the way reluctantly. On the moors there are often great semi-circles dug out right out of the rises in the ground – and hollowed out round the sides, leaving an overhanging ridge – under this the sheep group, to shelter from the wind, rain or sun – or to sleep. They seem to like to lie against something, a wall, or a big stone.

July 22nd 1927.

From Birnam to Melrose – This is the first day in Scotland that I have seen no Gulls. On the moors I saw several Plover and Grouse, and fishing in a river near the road a young Heron. I was able to have a good look at it as it rose up out of the water, and flew in the direction in which we were going, its long neck first outstretched, then drawn into its body as it got well under way. It only went a short distance – then – as we stopped again to look at it, it flew back to where it had come from. I feel sure it was a young bird, as its plumage had a mottled appearance, on the neck and under body, instead of being pure white. At Melrose I saw three Jackdaws sitting on a chimney top of our hotel – and swallows nesting in the Abbey. I have found no Ling Heather out. only Bell, and Cross Leaved. The latter is really the prettiest of all, being a very delicate pink, but the Bell Heather is very beautiful in the mass – as it is such a glorious carmine purple in the sunshine.

July 23rd

Impressions of the run from Melrose to Boroughbridge – Yorks.

"Many Beeches blown down by gales, lying like fallen giants. Curious green mound like hills – Bleak heights. Wonderful view over miles of country spread out like a map. Grazing sheep. Plovers. No Gulls anywhere. Wide borders of Scarlet Poppies on either side of the road – for miles flat country".

July 24th

**B**oroughbridge.

**W**atched Spotted Flycatchers feeding their young, and Whitethroats or "Nettle creepers" climbing tall grasses in the field.

July 25th

**L**outh to **K**ing's **L**ynn. "Very flat country, winding roads, with wide grass borders. Fields of waving green wheat, barley and oats, all in the ear. Fragrant cut hay. Blue sky, billowy white clouds – Canals. Blazing Sunshine and heat". At King's Lynn I saw a Yellow Hammer and in the harbour there were dozens of **starlings** on the fishing smacks picking up little bits of fish and cockles from the nets and decks. Most of them were young birds, a uniform **brown**, no white specks on the feathers, and quite unlike the parent birds. Their plumage does not change until end of July or August.

July 26th

**K**ing's **L**ynn to **T**ilbury. intensely green and turnips. Wonderful Canals with high dykes. of yellowing Corn. River Thames. and

Very flat low lying country fields of potatoes tall weeping Elms. Windmills. Fields Hollyhocks. hundreds of Gulls.

July 27th

**A**t **R**ochester I saw Jackdaws in the old Castle – and two Brown-headed Gulls were seated among the pigeons which were feeding on the lawn, – surrounded by playing children –

July 29th 1927.

Saw a Yellow Hammer, flying along the road - in Kent -

August 1st

Fernhurst.

Marsh Tits have appeared again. They have been very
scarce round here lately, though last year a
good many came- Rather like the Cole Tit in
size and colour- but with a very black head - a
pretty graceful little bird. The wettest of wet days.
but a bright starlight night.

August 2nd

A glorious day. Found Campions in the Upper
field, and one mulberry on our new tiny tree.
There are many Small Tortoiseshell Butterflies
about. two have been hung up on ceilings in
the house for some time, probably because it
has been so cold, but now they have gone off again.
I frequently see pairs of white butter- flies flitting
about-close together. but I can never catch them settled down, to
see what they are. Another starlight night. Tiny thumb-
nail moon.

August 3rd.

Wonderful Summer's day. Blue sky, hot sun. I saw my first
Dragonfly of the year. darting about in the lane. - its
long green irridescent body glinting
in the sunshine. Polue Tits are
growing tamer, one hung on the open window by one leg! They
always take away the largest pieces of bread., whereas the
larger birds Take the smaller, or eat them on the spot.
.Again a lovely starlight night.

**August 4th.**

Today I saw five different kinds of birds on the shelter at the same time - A Blue Tit on the Cocoanut, a Robin and a Chaffinch on the Tray. and a Nuthatch and Great Tit on the basket of fat beneath. Young Robins are constantly getting in under the fruit cage. and having to be got out with much difficulty.

**August 5th**

Saw quantities of butterflies. one flew very curiously, rising and falling unevenly and I found it to be a "Large White" with a big piece out of the left front wing. The Female of the Large White has two black spots on the front wing. Saw many "Common" "Blue" couples. The males are lilac blue all over. except for a white margin—the females are slightly brown, and have row of orange spots in the margin. "Peacocks" and "Small Tortoiseshells" were resting with wide spread wings on the grass. I think I saw "Clifton Blue" blue on the upper surface and grey brown on the lower, covered with tiny black spots, edged with white.

**August 6th**

This morning a wasp got entangled in a spiders web on my window. The spider darted out, but was afraid to venture too near. and the next moment the wasp had freed itself and flown away- The spider retired discomfited.

**Pagham.**

**August. 10th**

Found Small Bindweed in the lane leading to our camp. - a great deal of it everywhere. The bud is wonderfully folded. rather like an umbrella. The stem is very twisted —

August 11th 1927.

Saw Vipers Bugloss Thistles _ these and the air. Saw down by the sea. also Marsh Plume have several heads on each stalk generally one flower is seeding before the last is fairly out. and the woolly down is floating about in the air. Saw a flight of Cormorants.

August 16th

Many butterflies on the way down to the beach. There are a great many Wall Butterflies; they are beautifully marked. and look like patches of dappled sunlight and shadow.
We have quantities of wasps in camp, which always gather round us at meals. There are also a great many earwigs. one wonders where They all come from.

August. 19th

While at tea down by the lagoon, watched two lovely white Swans. with their four baby cygnets. I think they are Whooper Swans. and the cygnets are dark grey brown. Found a Horned in the marsh. Yellow Poppy

August 18th

Found very curious Seaweed on the beach like a bead necklace. I believe it is Sea Wrack. at Bognor. rather called Knotty

August 22nd

A tre- men- dous gale blowing. The blown off the field. Later the wind night was calm. Camp was nearly dropped and the

**A** lovely day - glorious starlight night. and so absolutely still -

**W**oke to another lovely day; it was very cold at early dawn, and everything was covered with a fine white frost. Pink sunrise -

Fernhurst.

**S**aw a Red Admiral the first I have also Woodpecker on tree - Could not see it very was a green one - as with a red head. and it wings as the Lesser Spotted Woodpecker has.

Butterfly in the lane seen this year. and the old chestnut clearly, but think it it was a large bird had no white in the

**I**n the field found a very tiny frog, and all kinds of Toadstools and fungus. One fungus was on a stick - a white woolly mass,     mauve and sticky inside.   also cotton wool mould  on moss -
Some of the Toadstools    are very pretty    - Mauve
ones,    Red    ones,   and tiny min-   iature
groups    about    inch high.   a   double
Yellow    Toadstool   -    Puff balls
Found    Dog Violets still in bloom..    also ripe
Blackberries,    and Vipers Bugloss -

**F**ound a Pigmy Shrew Mouse in the garden.    it is a tiny little thing with a very long  pointed nose. which    it wriggles perpetually.

**H**ad a beautiful Peacock Butterfly in my  window.

September 2nd 1927.

Found young green acorns on the oaks in the field and dozens of baby Frogs in the grass. Also Jays feathers wing ones, barred with blue and white. Gathered Black- berries for a tart- There are still many only in bloom as yet. Found more curious Toadstools. One was dark brown on top - and instead of being ribbed underneath, was full of tiny holes like a sponge. And when broken it became suffused with bright purple. A great deal of Agrimony (Common) still out. Found my first Hazel Nut of the season, also Common English Meadow Grasshopper. very bright green, and hardly disting- uishable from the grass it was sitting on. Saw a very curious Spider in the house- its body was round, about the size of a pea, pinky brown. and its legs were very fine, and quite 2 inches long.

September 3rd

Caught a White Ermine Moth on the stairs, at first its wings were so folded that I could not see its hinder wings or body at all-, but when I put it under an inverted tumbler, it most obligingly spread its wings and flew up and down the glass. The hinder wings are pure white, and the front ones tinged cream- the body speckled with rows of tiny black bars.

September 7th

Virginia Creeper is everywhere turning a glorious deep red- Missel Thrushes are very busy eating the ripe berries from our May Trees. We are inundated with wasps which are now at their sleepy crawly stage.

September 9th

Found a beautiful Moth on my ceiling last night, and caught it in a tumbler to ex- amine by day. Cannot find it in my butterfly & Moth book. It appeared at first to have no antennae, but I found that these were neatly folded back at the side of the face. Having

"Herald Moth."

drawn its portrait. I took it out and put it on the terrace wall. it fluttered its wings for a moment, and then flew on to the porch clematis, where it suspended itself upside down on the under side of a leaf - it looked exactly like the withered leaves round it.  Saw a fascinating spider in the garden. black with white stripes round it. legs also striped. It had a wonderful web. Looked to me like a Hunting Spider, yet this spider is supposed to have no web. so I cannot understand what it was. At 7.15 pm there was a glorious sunset and the hill opposite was brilliantly lit with golden sunlight, and everything glowed like burnished brass.

September 11th

There are quan- ti- ties of Small Scabious in our wild garden. and they are very popular with the Humble Bees. of which there seem to be many kinds - some are brown, some black- and orange. Some are very fluffy and silvery. these are the prettiest. not nearly as large as the big brown. but much more delicate.

September 15th

Have heard the owls a great deal lately at night. calling to each other across the valley. one sits in a tree quite close to my window, by its shrill cry of ki-wit - ki-wak I think it must be a Tawny Owl.

September 17th

There is a constant cooing of Ring Doves, or Wood Pigeons up in the Copse. They sit in the fir trees, coo-cooing by the hour, and I have seen them flying up from the wood.

September 18th

Looking out of my window in the early morning after a wet night I saw crowds of birds, pecking about on the Lawn. Robins chirping their loud and cheerful chirp. -Blackbirds flirting their long tails as they alighted - they were very busy in the elder bush, where the berries are almost ripe - Missel Thrushes. which are much bigger than the Song Thrush. and even Blackbird - being eleven inches in length - It is a greyer brown than the S. Thrush - and has a good deal of white in the under body. - I saw Tits of all kinds flitting about the pergola, clinging to the wood- work, and pecking for small insects. The Nuthatch too, with his little tz - tz - and Chaffinches.

September 19th.<br>1927.

The flowers are very draggled and sad looking after so much rain-
    Trees are taking on their autumn tints, and leaves are beginning
to fall.   Roses in the garden are still quite lovely. I sometimes find such
odd looking                           Spiders in the house. with tiny bodies, and legs

from one and Harvester.   a half to two inches long. there was one on
my wall this                         morning, it walked very slowly, and
felt every step                       with its long hair like legs. each leg had
two joints.                          and the body & legs were a pale red brown.
A flight of Swallows passed over the house this morning, wheeling and circling
over our heads- and I saw more at about 6 in the evening, rather
scattered.  These are the first I have seen this year migrating.

September. 22nd

A terribly wet and windy night; many plants in the garden broken and beaten
down. Everything too wet to pick.

September 23rd

Early morning was fine, and the Sun quite hot.  Later in the day there
was a torrential downpour

September 24th

Lovely day and warm in the sun.  At about 5.30 there was an "April
    Shower" with the sun shining, lighting the trees with a glorious golden
brilliance; then came a wonderful double Rainbow, and the inner bow
had what I have never seen before, three narrow double rims of mauve

and blue on the under side. It lasted for quite a long time – Cold evening

September 25th.

A heavenly morning – a light frost in the night. As yesterday we had a shower about 5.30 p.m. and another double rainbow, but the second one was rather faint.

September 26th

Polly and the cats very amusing together. When Martie settles himself to sleep on the windowsill, Polly insists on sitting by him, and converses gently with him. but Martie turns a deaf ear to all his blandishments. Polly then nibbles very carefully all round his ears – When I throw Nieco a piece of toast he always turns it into a mouse, by chasing it along the floor for a time, finally he picks it up in one paw, and hands it into his mouth! At 3.30 there was a sharp shower and a Hail storm, it was icey cold.

September 27th.

Frost in the night. It was very cold in the garden before breakfast. Such a glorious day. There were two lovely Red Admiral butterflies on a clump of Michaelmas Daisies; they stayed there for ages, and I was able to photograph them. Found an enormous Crane Fly, or Daddy-Long-Legs, in the house. but am doubtful if it was really a Crane Fly. as the body was differently shaped. and the legs not placed the same way on the body. The front pair came from under the chin, and the two back ones from the centre of the fat part of the body.

October 3rd

Such a lovely day. Brimstone butterflies were flitting about the nasturtiums I saw Swans and wild duck on Frensham Ponds. Noticed that many of the Pine trees instead of growing up in one single trunk, are forked about fifteen feet from the top.

October 2.nd.

The end of "Summer Time." A drizzly dull dark day.

October 4th 1927.

**A** Queen Wasp came buzzing into my room early, but flew out again before I could kill it. C.M.S killed one in her room. The Mosquitos, or "Common Gnats" are very plentiful this year, I suppose owing to all the damp weather we have had. It is the female only which bites – and which make the ping-ing noise, with its wings, and breathing apparatus.

October 6th

**T** he fourth lovely day we have had. Butterflies flitting in the sunshine. Red Admiral – Brimstone, and Small Tortoiseshell. A few belated Wasps still about, in a very sleepy state.

October 7th

**L** ovely day again. Autumn tints glorious. Bracken russet brown, Poplars with golden leaves flashing in the sunshine. Chestnuts red and gold. At Southampton a thick mist fell, and the sea was still like glass.

October 8th

**F** rance.

**T** here was a thick fog all night in the Channel. From the train, going to Paris. I saw hundreds of apple trees, laden with apples, green yellow and red. We passed and repassed along the banks of the Seine, every tree and branch mirrored in its unbroken surface. Everything veiled in delicate sunlit mist, and the grass sparkling with dew.

October 9th.

**A** utumn is much more advanced here than at home. Many of the Horse Chestnut trees are completely leafless, also the Plane trees. Some of the Poplars in the Bois de Boulogne were lovely, the wind in the branches made the leaves shimmer like Golden Coins in the sunlight.

October 10th

**F** ed the Sparrows in the Tuileries, with crumbs, they are wonderfully tame – They vary very much in colour, and neckties – some light brown, some red brown, and some very dark brown. Some

were Tree                                    Sparrows with dark patches in the
centre of                                    the white cheeks, and very small neck
ties.

**A**gain fed the Sparrows in the Tuileries.
They are                          not very sharp sighted, as they never
seem to notice the crumbs on the ground, only the pieces actually thrown
to them – They stand with their heads on one side, waiting for the
next piece, with any amount already at their feet.   Saw on two
occasions a very tiny brown Butterfly or Moth flitting by – about half an
inch across – it passed so quickly I had not time to inspect it properly.

**E**ngland –                                            October 13th

**G**rey and drizzling at early dawn, and very cold coming into Southampton
Harbour. All leaves changing colour, and falling, but no trees bare
as yet.   As I came in at the front gate          a Grey Wagtail rose up from
the lily pond, and flew round for a                      Time –
He has a very long tail, longer than the
Pied Wagtail, and is even more lively in his
jerky movements. Grey on the top of the head              and back.
and bright yellow on the under parts. A very              pretty bird.
I notice a great difference in the garden after              even a few
days absence. The weather has been Sunny, and the beds are quite gay
with Dahlias Chrysanthemums, Michaelmas Daisies and Roses. A
Cock Pheasant and two Hens paraded along the top of the Yew hedge for
a long time. Small birds are very busy in the newly dug Rose beds. I
saw a Cole Tit, the first since Spring, on the bird shelter.

October 14th

**N**o wasps round here now – but in Haslemere I saw several in a
confectioners window. Saw a Wood Pigeon close up, in a tree in

the lane – it was very grey in Colour.

October 15th 1927.

There was a Peacock Butterfly in my window – very faded – and ragged at the edges of the wings – Let it out into the sunshine.

October 16th

Passed many wonderfully coloured trees on our way to Milford. In many places the chestnut leaves were pure yellow, like lemons shading to orange and red. and we saw one tree that looked as if it were on fire, with vivid crimson and pink leaves. – It looked like a wild cherry. The Punch Bowl was red-brown and gold against a sky of intense blue, with fleecy clouds.

October 17th

The Pear Trees are loosing their leaves very fast. – They swish swish through the air, and fall crisply on each other. When I looked out of my window at 10.30 pm I saw a "Shooting Star" it seemed to dart across the sky over Blackdown, with a long tail of sparks behind it.

October 19th

Nearly all the leaves have gone off the rose trees – earlier I think than usual. Alberic Barbier, climber is flowering again – and several Clematis, (Sensation, Ville de Lyon, r Belle Nantaise) are in full bloom.

October 20th

(19th)
Leant out of my window last thing at night. Stars shining brightly and the still night air filled with the faint persistant rustle of falling leaves. Found a large Black Beetle under a rock rose I was clipping     I do not know what kind it was, certainly not a "Stag", though     it was a large one. It scuttled away very quickly.

October 21st

Found a curious little mothlike creature on the ceiling, when the wings were folded, it was like an aeroplane. spread out the front wings were yellow brown, the back ones like fine fluffy feathers, rather grey.

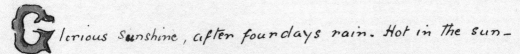

Plume

October 22nd

Such a wet day. until about 3 P.M. when the sun came out, and everything was bathed in golden light. The wet fallen beech leaves made a glowing red-brown carpet. and the trees with their many tinted leaves, were glorious in the sunshine.

October 24th

Every morning at 7o/c a Wren sings under my window for about five minutes - and then comes a Robin, and makes a great fuss about something, always behind a bush where I cannot see him.

October 26th

How dirty London seems after the country! even the very sparrows are grimey little fellows. But the trees in the parks are lovely. A windy day - and the air full of scurrying leaves and dust.

October 28th

A terribly wet day, but at 4 p.m. it cleared. and the sky was wonderful. great fleecy grey clouds drifted by, gradually changing to brassy yellow, then to delicate shell pink, this faded to misty blue grey, and night fell.

October 29th

Glorious sunshine, after four days rain. Hot in the sun -

Found a pretty little moth on the drawingroom floor, and think it must be a Winter Moth, male — It refused absolutely to spread its wings, which were red-brown, like a piece of bark but it had a distinct little black spot on each front wing. The female of the Winter Moth is like a grub and wing- less.

Today, coming home up the lane I saw crowds of Tits in a big Oak tree. Then suddenly I noticed among them several Long Tailed Tits. This is the first time I have ever seen them in my life. I cannot think why They never come to our shelter with the other Tits - or even into our garden. They were high up in the tree, and against the light. so I could not see them as well as I could have wished. In the copse I surprised two large fat Rabbits feeding quite near the road. I "froze" They sat up on their hind quarters and twitched their noses at me. then went lippety loppety down among the trees, their white tails bobbing up and down — Such a lovely afternoon, after heavy showers. Sun shining on the wet green lichened tree trunks. Blue sky and red-gold leaves reflected in every puddle. Carpets of beech leaves. Delicate pink and mauve lights on the hills. and Birds singing every where.

Weather wonderfully warm for the time of year. Masses of Dahlias still out in Hyde Park. Grey drizzling day. and thick fog in patches after dark.

Saw a belated wasp in a confectioners window in Haslemere. — There are two Small Tortoiseshell Butterflies hung up in the house, sleeping soundly. Now that the lily leaves are dying off in the pond, the goldfish are making their reappearance. They have grown tremendously during the summer. One which was bright gold, with a singularly bright band round the base of the tail, was in hiding for about a month, and emerged silver, with a vivid silver band round the tail.

**O**wls were calling calling to each other across the valley just before Sun-up. and then cocks started to crow - The air was curiously still, and the sky grey and brooding. Puck lay in the den window, watching the Bluebottles which swarm in hundreds on The Ivy which has just finished flowering, the berries have not yet begun to turn black; it is "Common Ivy" and the main Stem is very thick and old. The small Stems cling To The wall by means of tiny roots or tendrils which grow here and there on the under side Many birds came for crumbs at breakfast. - a Tree Sparrow blackbirds, chaffinches etc. Much colder towards even- ing - and later bright moonlight and stars.

November 6th

**T**he Plum Tree at the back gate is flowering in patches, it has a habit of late-flowering like this. A cold bleak day - I

November 7th

**P**lanted bulbs in the grass. Great long pink worms kept emerging, there seemed to be no end to their length. some were 8 to 10 in long.

November 8th

**A** bitterly cold day. Sharp white frost in the night. Towards midday very foggy. In the evening a breeze sprang up; the fog lifted, and the air became a little warmer. Rain in the night.

November 10th

**F**reezing day at 7 pm a few flakes of snow fell. Brilliant moonlight night.

November 11th

**S**harp ground frost. the first Bullfinch in till the 28th of this Tree . A Cole → away a large All the Dahlias have gone black. Saw the Spirea Tree ; last year They did not come month when all the leaves were off The Tit came at breakfast, and took piece of bread. He is a tiny little

fellow, and looks smaller than the Marsh Tit, though really the same size — He
is distinguishable from the Marsh Tit by his white cheeks, and white patch
on the nape of the neck — He seems to go away from here in the summer,
as I never see him in the summer months.

November 12<sup>th</sup> 1927.

**H**ard ground frost — Snow fell for about five minutes in the early morning.
Great Tits were very busy climbing about the dejected rose bushes. Every
thing looked pinched with cold — Towards 10am the sun came out and warm-
ed the air, and everything seemed to revive and sparkle in the sunshine.
The Oak Trees cling to their leaves, some are still quite green, others a glorious gold-
en brown. Oaks vary a great deal in shape, and growth — in some the branches
grow out quite horizontally, in others they slant up obliquely. Some are short
and squat, others tall and lanky. Their acorns too vary very much, some
being fat and round, others long and thin. most of them are beginning to sprout. They crack open at the pointed end, and the
shoot emerges and turns upward. some are quite red inside.
The Hazels also cling to their leaves, which shrivel on
the boughs before they fall. They already have their next
years catkins and buds. Flocks of Starlings flew about
the fields — I saw two groups, one of about a hundred,
chattering and picking about in the grass. Found
the bright scarlet berries of White Bryony in the
hedges. and two belated Buttercups in the field

November 13<sup>th</sup>

**I**t snowed for some time in the morning, but
Such wet snow that it did not lie at all.
While I was planting bulbs in the afternoon a fat
Robin came and sat with me, perching on the
bulb bags, and hopping about the newly turned earth.
One moment I saw him with a worm quite two inches long,
the next instant it had gone com- pletely.' he then sat
in the Holly tree and sang to me.

November 15<sup>th</sup>

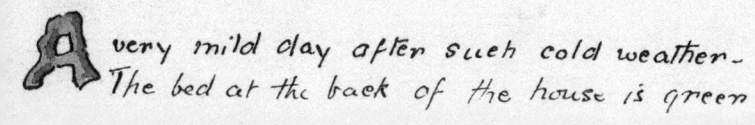

**A** very mild day after such cold weather — quite hot in the sun.
The bed at the back of the house is green with poppy seedlings.

November 17th.

Found many green grubs in the earth while I was planting bulbs. They lie curled up about one to two inches under the ground, and are like fat green hairless caterpillars. A Robin hopped round me as usual. He sees spiders in the bags of bulbs, but never dares to take the plunge in!

November 18th

A Robin comes on the new cocoanut, which is hung sideways, so he sits on the top, as on a log, and leans over to peck at the end - often overbalancing in the attempt.!

November 19th.

Such a wet day, wind and rain all night, and the day dark and misty. All the leaves are now off the Spirea tree, but no sign of the Bullfinches. The one which came on the 11th must have been sent ahead to see if the seeds were ripe, and he evidently found they were not so!

November 20th

Rain, rain, rain. a Robin had a tremendous bath in the birds bowl, getting right down into it several times, in really deep water, and splashing about a great deal.

November 22nd

A Pair of Bullfinches appeared in the Spirea Tree this morning, but the seeds were either too sodden with rain, or not ripe enough, for they sat there not eating anything, and soon went away again. A flight of Pigeons passed over the house at about 2 pm. Quite warm in the evening, and moths were fluttering round the light at the front gate. Jasmini Nudiflorum is in full bloom, and the apple blossom pink Pyrus Japonica is covered with buds, many in flower.

November 23rd

Very misty. Arrived in London 10.50 AM. to find it in complete darkness. This was due to accumulation of smoke in the upper atmosphere - the air above being warmer than the air beneath, the smoke was unable to disperse. There was no fog in the streets.

November 25th

A glorious day of sunshine.

November 26th 1927.

A lovely morning followed by intervals of sunshine and mist. At one time the whole valley was enveloped in a thick white fog, only a thin line of far horizon showing - it looked like an immense lake, and had a wonderful Japanese effect.

November 27th

Thick mist all day. I never saw so many birds on the shelter - there was a constant flow of them - the Blackbirds are quite tiresome, they eat the fat at such a rate, and keep off the smaller birds - One blackbird who had a large piece of bread kept chasing another, why I couldn't make out, as the one being chased evidently had no wish for the bread. Finally they had a tremendous fight on the path. No sign of the bullfinches. - In the woods all was still, hardly a sound was to be heard. only the drip drip of the moisture from the trees, the rustle of the falling leaves, and the occasional raucous cry of a Pheasant in the far distance.

November 28th.

Our Robin has learnt to balance nicely on top of the cocoanut and can even cling to one end, but rather precariously.

November 29th

Pouring rain from morning till night. In London it was very dark for some hours, due to the smoke being unable to disperse.

December 1st

A Mistle-Thrush sits about sadly in the Orchard, very puffed out with cold, and looking so lonely, he may be suffering from indigestion, from the many Holly berries he has eaten. Hazel leaves are few on the branches now, but vivid green and lemon yellow, so that they look like blossoms in the hedges. Many Oaks are still thickly covered with leaves.

December 4th

Such a bleak foggy day. In the lane, I met a Blackbird - he was making such a fuss, and for no apparent reason; he kept up a continual cry, hopped across the road, and disappeared, still crying, into the copse. He was practically the only bird I saw. The others must have gone to roost early, it was so dark and cold.

December 5th

The Tits congregate in numbers in the plum tree at the back gate. Every time anyone goes near G.M.S's window, there is a flutter of wings, and several Tits appear on the sill, and in the branches nearest the window.

December 6th

A glorious day of sunshine. The Wrens are very noisy and quarrelsome in the early morning, I hear a constant angry tit-it-it — and then bursts of song. Saw a Weasel run leisurely across the main road, he paused for a moment in the hedge, looking at us, then disappeared. The day began with a lovely sunrise, and ended with a red gold sunset.

December 7th

Brilliant sunshine in the morning — Fog all the way from Hindhead to Church Crookham; in patches it was almost quite clear. Saw many rabbits on Frensham common, they scuttled away from the lights of the car. While waiting on the Village Green at 8.30 heard Brown Owls crying to each other in the distant woods.

December 8th

Misty all day, so we were unable to see the eclipse of the Moon.

December 9th

Brambles are mostly still are turning red and yellow. until the Spring, making in the Sunshine, and vivid quite green. A few in the lane. The Beech hedges keep their leaves glorious patches of golden brown copper in the rain.

December 11th

Such a gale in the night. and still blowing during the day. Very bleak and icey cold.

December 12th

Watched a Blackbird eating a very fat worm about three inches long. He siezed it by the middle, and shook it violently, then put it down

and rested, after which he shook it again; then he refreshed himself with a holly berry — Then continued shaking the worm, till finally it came in
halves. He swallowed them down in two great gulps, and took a long
rest before turning his attentions to the finding of crumbs. A very bleak
cold day, with an icey wind blowing — Sunshine in the morning.

December 14th, 27.

Raining all day. Much warmer.

December 15th

Slight fog. and very cold. Saw dozens of Moorhen on Frensham
Ponds, as we passed by — and
two Whooper Swans in the water under the
Tilford Bridge — The first Starlight night for many a night.

December 16th

Icey Cold. It began to snow at 8AM. and continued for about an hour, till
there was a fine layer on the Ground. Then it ceased and the Sun came
out brilliantly. May Thorn berries very plentiful in the
hedges near Godalming. At Pease- marsh we left the
sunshine behind us. and Guildford was dark and cheer-
less. Dogs eyes in the dark, when the car lights shine on
them are like tiny round phosphorescent lamps — some glowing
red, some green.

December 17th

A hard frost during the night. Lily pond frozen over, yesterdays snow
still on the ground — Icey cold all day. At 4.15 heard Wrens singing outside my east window, and look-
ing out saw four or five searching
for a roosting place in the ivy — They
made a great deal of noise, rustling
and crackling the stiff ivy leaves — then suddenly
all flew off to the big Ash Tree, where they hopped about
for some time, singing — Next they visited the South wall and the roof
of the porch — but finally they came back to the East wall, where I think they
settled for the night. A Robin too was fluttering in the ivy and on the low wall.
he was annoyed to find me watching him, and flew off in high dudgeon, uttering little shrill chirps. Still, cold, starlight night.

Hard frost in the night. Everything looked pinched and dejected with cold. The sun rose over Blackdown like a great ball of fire. Crowds of birds came for crumbs, very puffed out with cold, among them a Hedge Sparrow (Accentor) which has not been for many months. No further sign of the Bullfinches. I think they cannot be coming to the Spirea this year.

December 19<sup>th</sup>

Bitterly cold night, and blowing hard. Snow fell between 8 & 10 AM. Then the Sun came out and the day was fine though intensely cold. Birds flocked to the shelter all day long. A Hen Blackbird established herself on the fat and kept all the small birds away, so I hung up a bag of it under the roof and the Tits highly approved, a Blue Tit being the first to sample it. Every thing frozen. the leaves of the evergreens hang down limp and dejected.

December 20<sup>th</sup>

Terribly cold all day, towards evening the wind rose and it blew a gale.

December 21<sup>st</sup>

Shortest day of the year. In the night the weather changed. Rain came down in torrents, and the wet on the frozen roads turned to ice and traffic was impossible till about 9.30 AM. when it began to thaw It poured with rain off and on all day. Much warmer.

December 22<sup>nd</sup>

Deluges of rain during the night and at intervals during the day. Quite warm. First Snowdrop out in the garden.

December 23<sup>rd</sup>

Very mild, rain at intervals all day. The Holly Tree has not been denuded of berries this year as it was last. I think the bird shelter is such an attraction, and the Blackbirds love the fat. Collected mosses to make a village in a bowl. there are many different species in the garden. The fine short kind which grows on the rocks, has the most fascinating Lichens growing on it. "Pixie Cups" of palest grey green, and another rather like it, but with no cup, and curly stems Fern moss is very pretty, and the wavy hair moss is covered with spore capsules.

Made a Christmas Tree for for the birds. T. got me a tree from the woods and planted it in a pot. I put it on the terrace wall, and hung on it, 2 rings of cocoanut- one end of same- 2 lumps of fat. and 2 bones. To the topmost bough I fixed the second cocoanut end upside down, cleaned out and filled with hemp and sunflower seeds. The birds were a little shy at first - a Blue Tit was the first to come, then a Marsh Tit, more Blue Tits and the Robin Much as I love the Robin I wish he were not so aggressive - several times he frighten- ed the Blue Tit from the seeds, by flying down at him from the Holly Tree. He himself reached the lowest lump of fat by jumping at it. it didn't occur to him to sit on the branch above..! Weather so mild that I sat at my open window sewing, and watching the birds on the green.

December 25th

Rain, rain, rain - very mild, almost warm, and quite unseasonable. The miniature hyacinths I planted on Nov 6. are now over an inch high. and today the leaves have parked, showing the flower buds. The birds are delighted with the Christmas Tree, and today came the Nuthatch - he stood below on the wall. craned his neck up, to see, then jumped on to the trunk, and ran up and down it. sampling both lumps of fat. One Blue Tit tried a bone. but they all prefer the fat. Found a curious Fly outside my window. eating crumbs of biscuits. it had very strongly lined opalescent wings - and an enormous pro- bosis with a trumpet like tip, into which he sucked the crumbs - but he did not seem to swallow them. At 9.30 P.M. There was quite an inch and a half of snow on the ground, and it was blowing hard.

Diptera
Labenlind

December 26th

It blew a gale all night. and snowed. The ground was white in the morning and it continued blowing and snowing all day. Birds came in flocks to be fed, the moment I went near the window, they hovered in front of it. Their tree had been blown down in the night. and buried beneath a drift of snow. I dug it out, and stood it up by a bush, shaking the snow from the boughs - it was soon blown down again; but the birds crowded over it all day long. - The Pied Wagtail reappeared, looking very cold and hungry. The Robin was most aggressive all day long. and the Great Tits were rather quarrelsome among themselves. The Cats went out reluctantly, and came in covered with snow, shaking their paws in disgust Still blowing a gale at 11. p.m.

December 27th 1927.

About 8 to 10 inches of snow on the ground, and much deeper in the drifts. Snow still falling, and North wind blowing. Creepers and trees bent beneath the weight of the snow. and great icicles hanging from the eaves. again on the of water came for the Birds' tree buried completely. H.T.S. put it up and birds flocked to it. Pied Wagtail early scene, and remained all day. Put out a dish and the Wagtail took a drink. A Starling very first time, but the other birds alarmed him and he flew off without getting anything to eat. Tits fought each other on the tree, and all the birds were more or less quarrelsome. A wren which had been creeping in and out the crevices on the wall, came and watched the other birds eating, but he would not venture near, he was almost blown away by the wind, as he sat on the top of the wall. Thaw set in during the morning, and large lumps of snow fell from the Holly tree, and there was a continual drip drip from the icicles. Wind rose towards the evening and it grew very cold. Found an earwig on my diary!

December 28th

Freezing hard all night- and the water I put out for the birds at 9.AM froze in half an hour. A terrible tragedy occurred in the morning, I was writing in my room when something impelled me to go into the drawingroom to look down at the birds tree. The Pied Wagtail was strutting round it, picking about in the snow, suddenly something black leapt out and was on him - I opened the window and shouted at Nicco - he ran down the steps with the bird in his mouth. I flew down and out of the diningroom, when he saw me coming Nicco dropped the poor little Wagtail - but alas. he was dead. This is the first time I have known one of the cats to touch a bird on the terrace. Later I gave Nicco a beating, and he was very ashamed. Tree covered with birds all day. Six on it at one time. and another Pied Wagtail appeared. perhaps the mate of the first one, there were never two there at the same time. I cleared a space on the grass round the shelter, and many birds congregated there, including an ill-kempt starling who ate voraciously. Saw a flock of starlings wheeling over the house. They have a curious way of flying, beating their wings rapidly, then ceasing, and planing for a second or two - but in rather a jerky manner. The Hedge Sparrow came he always picks about on the ground, and never tries the tree. In the afternoon it was thawing fast, a rain of drips from the icicles fell continuously on my window sill. Very cold towards evening, freezing at night-

December 29th 1927.

It blew all night, and the morning was grey - it looked like more snow, but the sky cleared. The sun came out, and a quick thaw set in. Many birds came early, then, in the afternoon there were hardly any on the tree, as the ground was beginning to reappear in places, and they were off to other hunting grounds. The Robin has become very proficient in hanging on to the cocoanuts - he does it so well I sometimes mistake him for a Tit at the first glance. Colder towards evening, and freezing at night. Misty Moon.

December 30th

Wind dropped completely in the night, but still freezing. Birds still very hungry for crumbs. Saw two Robins fighting over a large piece of bread at the back of the house. The Chaffinches are the best tempered of all the birds, especially the hens which are very gentle and retiring. Saw many starlings, pecking about the ground in a garden in the village. The snow is rapidly melting away, but roads are very slippery. The laurels have shed a quantity of leaves in the gales, and the lawn is dotted all over with them sticking up in the snow, at a distance they look like birds feeding. Threw a piece of cocoanut out of window, and later saw a Robin enjoying it, until was chased away by another Robin. how very quarrelsome they are. Bitterly cold in the evening.

December 31st.

The early morning was grey and chill. Roads on the way to London very bad with snow. Near Milford saw Gypsies Ponies scraping the snow away to get at the grass, and one was shaking the snow from the hedge, and eating green bramble leaves. There was skating on the Wisley Pond. Saw many boughs broken off with the weight of the snow. The Hammersmith reservoir was partly frozen over, and Gulls were standing folornly about on the ice. At 4 pm it began to snow again. and continued for about two hours _ A cold night.

# THE
# SECOND JOURNAL

1ST JANUARY 1928

TO

31ST DECEMBER 1928

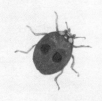

*The caption in Margaret's photograph album reads:*
*"M.G.S. as Margaret of Anjou,*
*Historical Fancy Dress Dance, 1st August 1911."*

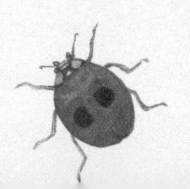

# 1928

(London)

**A** grey day. very slushy underfoot. Air damp and cold. Warmer towards evening - and thawing fast.

January 2nd

**R**ain nearly all day - clear at night.

January 3rd

**S**lightly foggy and raw - drizzling in the afternoon & evening.

January 4th

**L**ovely day, every thing bright in the sunshine. the Thames sparkling, and the Gulls wings gleaming white. saw none but Common Gulls.

January 6th

**V**ery strong Westerly gale blowing - Trees bending, dead leaves hurrying, and scurrying. A few flakes of snow fell. Parks very pretty - noticed old nests in the bare trees.

January 7th

(Fernhurst)

**D**rizzle in the early morning. Near Wimbledon a little copse of Silver Birches looked so pretty, with its carpet of silver green grass sparkling with dew. Noticed Trees down after the gale. The wind had abated, and at Haslemere we ran into thick mist. There are still a few patches of snow left where there were big drifts. The water in the Lily Pond has turned a curious milky blue, as if soft soap had been put in it, and the fish show up very plainly. They all came to the surface - eight of them. The dark one is missing - I have not seen him for months.

January 8th

**C**ounted more than a dozen aconites in the rock beds. More Snowdrops are appearing, and crocuses are showing their leaves. The Christmas Roses are badly eaten by slugs. A good many primroses are out in the rock beds and on the walls. Put fresh fat, a bone, and seeds on the birds tree - and staked it up - A Robin came at once to the seeds. Very few birds have been for crumbs. I suppose they find too much else-where now the ground is clear. Weather very mild. went in the garden without a coat. Sheep feeding in the field off the lane, one black one among them. Still night. moon in a soft haze.

January 9th 1928.

Saw the Ring Dove in the lane, he is always at the same spot, either feeding on the ground, or sitting up in a tree. The most glorious moonlight night, and absolutely still. so still that I could hear the rippling of the brook down in the valley.

January 10th

From sunshine to pouring rain and a gale of wind; then sudden still-ness, and a night of a myriad stars, and a great silver moon. Air very mild.

January. 11th

A deluge of rain in the early morning, followed by brilliant sunshine, which turned the world into Fairyland. every twig was hung with rows of glittering dancing rain-drops, and the dark washed green of Ivy and evergreens stood out against the grey lichened trunks of the oaks. the sky was blue, with little scudding white clouds. The night was cold and still, with bright moonlight and stars.

January 12th

White frost. At early dawn I heard a Brown Owl hooting close by. and saw him sitting silhouetted against the sky, in an oak tree opposite my window. after a minute he flew noiselessly away up the valley. The sunrise was glorious, and everything was bathed in rosy light. Later the wind rose and it poured with rain -

January 13th

Golden Sunrise. fine day. glorious sunset with dark clouds fringed with gold. As I was sitting in the car in Haslemere I saw a very curious Sparrow? feeding in the road with a band of Tree and House sparrows, it was rather more slender than the others, and a delicate silver grey. It's beak was exactly like that of a sparrow, but in build it more resembled a canary, It seemed quite at home with the Sparrows. for it flew away onto a roof with them, when startled by a passer-by. then returned with them to the road. One of the sparrows had lost his tail, and looked so funny.

January 14th 1928.

Dull morning with some mist. later wind and rain, and finally a bright still starlight night.

January 15th

A glorious day. On the way to Milford I noticed that many Oaks in the hedges had still a quantity of dead leaves clinging to the branches. I hung 2 strings of peanuts on the Christmas tree, and one on the shelter; and while I was out one nut was taken from the tree. The Marsh Tits sing every morning down in the wood. I stalked one in the lane, he was very busy with a berry which he got off a small bush; he wedged it into a branch in the hedge, and hammered away at it with his beak.

January 16th

Wet early morning. cleared about 10.30. Showers during afternoon. Lights very pretty. Watched a Great Tit eating the peanuts. He hauled up the string, hand over hand, and hammered at the nuts so hard with his beak that I thought he would over balance. He got in quite a temper with the sharp leaves which pricked him under the wings. He took about five minutes to get through the Shell, then flew triumphantly away into the holly tree with the kernel in his beak. The Marsh Tit also had a go at them, but soon went back to the fat. Glorious sunset. Sky golden and pink, and the sun went down like a great fiery red ball. One bell of Miniature white Hyacinth in bloom. planted Nov 21st.

January 17th

Gloriously fine, the first really springlike day. There was a frost in the night, and bird pools were lightly frozen over. At 6.30AM There was a crescent moon, and stars shining brightly. Owls were hooting in the valley. Then as the sun rose the Marsh Tits burst into joyous song. During the day the Sun was quite hot. Saw The Ring Dove in the lane. Put a spray of millet seed on the birds tree but none seemed to care much for it. The Great Tits love the Peanuts, and attack them with great vigour. Lovely starlight night.

**A** wretched day, rain and fog. On the way to London saw Swans and moorhen near Godalming. Country still very flooded.

January 19th

**G** lorious day again. Put out hemp seed in a small saucer on the bird shelter and soon saw the Marsh Tit come to it  He took seed after seed each time carrying it away to an apple tree, holding it in his claws and hammering it open with his beak. One miniature hyacinth entirely out – Took it out of bowl and repotted it in tiny pot – Several Bluebottles about the house and many flies out of doors in the sunshine – Saw two Chaffinches fighting in the hedge.

January 20th

**U** nceasing rain and fog. dank and cold – From the train on way to Lyndhurst saw some lambs which looked about three months old. Many Gulls near Southampton, and flocks of starlings and crows in fields.

January 21st

Lyndhurst.

**W** et early morning. clearing later, but not really fine. Went for tramps in the forest, and found many interesting things. Caddis Worms in a stream. The larva works itself into either a case of wood. or collects round itself a marvellous assortment of tiny stones, twigs, grains of etc, and makes a house in which it lives. sometimes it floats about, and at others cling to the stones at bottom of the stream. or to a plant. Polly-polly ferns growing on many of the trees, right up the trunks. Ferns do not produce ferns, but a Thallus, and the Thallus in its turn produces a fern. and so on. The forest is very damp, and the ground carpeted with wonderful mosses, the fern moss is the most beautiful. Lichen is on nearly all the trees, and in amongst the moss. Found Pixie cups, (pixidata) with red spores. Lichens have no roots or flowers, simply spores. We found Reindeer Lichen. which is the kind the reindeer eat in Siberia. Tree Beard Lichen. the plain rather flat kind, and its fruited variety, which is very pretty and like green daisies we found. Candle Snuff. Two curious Fungus which comes on dead wood only – and "Tremella", a curious substance very like a jelly fish, growing in a tree stump. Fungus consists chiefly of water. – Saw marble Galls on Oak leaves. and Artichoke Gall on a branch of yew. caused by insects which attack the trees; The Tree Then isolates the insect, by building a wall round it, and it very often gives off a substance The insect likes to feed on! When "Oak apples" come on the buds. They prevent the branches, + so do harm to The Tree.

January 22$^{nd}$

Lyndhurst.

Heavenly day. Went again to the forest. and studied birds. Heard the following. Song Thrush. Blackbird, Robin, Chaffinch. Blue Tit. Great Tit. Long Tailed Tit and Saw. Robin. Chaffinch. Blackbird, Great Tit. Marsh Tit Cole Tit . Long tailed Tit. Pigeon. Nuthatch . House sparrow. Blue Tit - Starling. and for the first time in my life a Tree Creeper. He was creeping up and up a very tall Tree, his tail bent against the trunk, and pecking peck- ing with his long curved down beak. We found shells of tiny nuts, like may berry kernels wedged in the bark of trees, evidently carried there by nuthatches, or Tits. Found Oak apples _ and in a stream tiny beetle like — animals were swimming a- bout. Found some bits of wood, green with fungus, cal- led Chlorosplenium Mycelium : in old days this was used for dyeing china _

January 23$^{rd}$

Lyndhurst.

Dull day with a good deal of rain . Saw flocks of Rooks feeding in a field on the way to the village. and saw and heard a song Thrush singing _

January. 24$^{th}$

Lyndhurst.

Very wet in the morning - later the sun came out and the afternoon was glorious _ Deep blue sky with sirrus and strata clouds reflected in the many marshy pools on the way to the pine wood The sun was setting, and the rosey light on The pine trunks , the bright green of the young trees, and in the distance the silver birches with their masses of delicate bare pink branches, made an unforgettable picture. Saw Minnows in a stream

January 25$^{th}$

Lyndhurst.

Fine day - Frosty in the early morning - found a clump of primroses in the wood _ Saw about three or four female Sparrows in the garden. these are like the male sparrows, without the necktie _ and have much redder and more pronounced markings on the back. also a buff streak over the eye. Have never noticed them before.

January 26th 1918.

Lyndhurst.

Saw a red squirrel on the outskirts of the wood. he ran down a tree and begun hunting for his store of food. digging first in one place _ Then another _ meanwhile a Tree Creeper was going up and up the Tree Trunk _ When it arrives at the top of a tree it flies down and begins again at The base. There are many Rooks in the field; and among them Jackdaws, and Wood-pigeons. Very wet afternoon.

January 27th

Lyndhurst _ Fernhurst.

Glorious morning . cloudy later . Apple buds on walls bursting into palest green leaves. From the train going to Haslemere saw several new born lambs

January 28th

A very wet day. Quite a lot of flowers out in the garden. Aconites, Snow-drops. Christmas Roses. etc . and the ground bristling with tulips, Narcissus, and daffodils _ yellow Crocus in full bud _

January 30th

Crowds of birds on tree and shelter. Great Tits and Marsh Tits very keen on hemps seeds _ almost fought over Them.

February 1st

Crocuses in bloom. Renewed the fat and cocoanuts on the birds tree, and the Tits flocked to it in numbers. One Marsh Tit is very bold, and when I have filled up the cocoanut shell with hemp- he is on it before I have moved five feet away: he takes as many as five and six in his beak and carries them off to a tree to eat.

February 2nd

Very cold. but a fine morning, some rain in the afternoon. later a gale got up, and there was a tremendous downpour of rain. Then quite sudden-ly everything was hushed, and there was a light fall of snow.

Cold and fine . beautiful moonlight night.

Wonderful sunrise - sky streaked with yellow, pink, and green, and before the sun came up in a blaze of gold - There was a great vertical ray of light up from the horizon - probably a reflection from the sea. Saw a squirrel on the outskirts of Haslemere. Late afternoon drizzle and fog. then a tremendous gale all night.

Strong South Westerly gale blowing - Deluges of rain - Fine afternoon. Garden very sodden with wet. Dug out and destroyed a large family of fourteen snails from a creviss in the wall, two of the shells were empty . Found two Scillas, out- and one plant of aubretia . also an Iris Stylosa. Erica Carnea in full bloom. Glorious sunset.

A heavenly day - Bright and warm Crocus spread wide their petals in the sun. -shine . Single arabis out.

Dull day. bleak and windy. Saw a Great Tit inspecting the Box nest on the pergola. He disappeared inside for about five minutes - then came up and sat in the doorway for a long time . Sparrow. (House) are contemplating building - several times they have come on my window sill, and have. inspected the ivy round it. All the birds are full of song, beginning about 6.45 AM. and going on till quite dark.

Found two frogs in the lily pond, the larger appeared to be dead, and the smaller one was sitting beside it ; but when I came with a net to fish them out, it quickly came alive . Threw them out by the pond in the lane. Cleaned out the Nuthatches nest in the porch. it was filled with beech leaves cut into rounds. and was sealed up with quantities of mud . Saw Blue Tits eating Hemp seeds, They eat them on the spot, wedging them in their claws, in- stead of carrying them away to a tree as the Marsh Tits do. The latter are

So greedy over them, that one of them stands in the dish, keeping the others out. then there is a fight, and all fly away. The Blue Tit also eats the Peanuts, waiting till the Marsh has pecked most of the shell away. Saw a Solitary Male Bullfinch in the Spirea Tree, pecking in a desultory way at the seeds, but with one eye on the hemp; he did not however dare to come so near the house and after a time flew away in the direction of the ponds. Found Laurel in bud — Hazel catkins loosening, and the tiny female flower with its fine crimson threads. or stigmas. This flower when fertilized by the pollen pro- duces either one or two nuts. Found Sallow (Palm) with its soft- silver catkin buds. In the fields the hedges are tufted with wool where the sheep have rubbed against them. The Primroses in the wood are in bud., and I found several in bloom.

February 10th 1929.

**M**ist, drizzle-rain and gale- finally snow, followed by a still starlight night. In the wood found Bluebell leaves up about two inches, and a good many primroses. The young Spanish chestnuts are being cut down, and the wood cleared. Was able to note the 8 rings of the 8 years growth. ( the wood is "cleared" every 7 or 8 years, and the young trees split for fencing. Each year the tree grows a fresh ring of wood under the bark, and if the year is wet the ring is wide- if very dry- narrow. Honeysuckle is covered with tiny green leaves.

February 11th

**P**alm out all along the road to Midhurst. Fine day but very windy. Oak tree in the lane split in halves at a fork, and lying across the road, having carried away the telephone wires. Renewed food on birds tree and shelter.

February 13th

**N**early every morning about 8.30 a large Cock Pheasant appears on the low wall; he struts along it, starting at every sound, walks across the lawn and often finishes his visit by parading along the top of the Yew Hedge. Every night a mole throws up a great mound of earth quite 8 or 9 inches high on the lawn.

February 14th

**F**rom my window saw a Rabbit in the garden. he must have jumped the wire somewhere. Went down to see if I could get him out. He ran under the beech hedge, and I think must have gone into the road, as the wire was low in places. Birds were very excited, and warned him with loud cries. Planted aubretia, rock roses etc on the new steps; and had four new nesting boxes put up. — Nuthatch on the old tree outside — Wren's or Tits on the Summer House. Tits outside my E window. and "anybirds" under the S. bay window. In the afternoon saw Nicco stalking the Cock Pheasant who was late with his daily visit. He walked down the outside of the hedge, while Nicco crawled along the inside - When he got on the wall Nicco could have had him easily. but was evidently afraid, he made a little run, and the pheasant jumped down into the road and disappear- ed among the trees while Nicco sat gazing after him. Dull day, turning to rain and drizzle. In the night it blew a gale.

February 16<sup>th</sup>

A raging westerly gale. and pouring rain - it cleared in the late afternoon and the night was still and starlit.

February 18<sup>th</sup>

Radiantly lovely day, brilliant sunshine - Frosty night. Birds singing at 6.30 AM. From early morn to dewey eve a Song Thrush warbled in a larch tree in our copse on the hill, and at sunset a Blackbird down in the valley sang a duet with him - Found the middle pond full of frog spawn in great jelly masses - The frogs were in a group in the centre and kept putting their heads up out of the water to look at me. A marvellous sunset, the whole sky tinged pink and tiny fleecy mauve clouds down on the south west horizon, woods and fields bathed in rosy light

February 19<sup>th</sup>

Another wonderful day of sunshine, tho' at times it clouded over for a few moments. Birds carolling joyously. Heard the nuthatch tapping tapping at the box nest on my S wall. and looking out I saw him sitting on the porch roof. Noticed the wood has been pecked away round the open- ing - am afraid he will find the nest rather small as it is meant for a tit. He evidently does not approve of the porch nest now the old rose and clematis have been cut down; and the new ones are too small to give any shelter.

February 20<sup>th</sup>

The Song Thrush was perched on the topmost bough of the Spruce tree from early morning singing joyously; and in the may tree the little Chaffinch was repeating his song over and over again. A Blue Tit was in the sallow by the pond, pecking busily at the "palm" buds. he seemed to be getting something from under the scaly brown leaf, I could hear it crack as he bent it back. ... were fighting under a bush ... bread. At Church Crookham saw ... lovely magpies on the road. their ... feathers and blue and green wings ... in the sunshine. Saw Rooks on Frensham ... A lovely pink sunset, the afterglow lasting ... time.

A Blue Tit and a Chaffinch ... for a piece of ... two ... white ... flashing ... Heath. ... for a long

February 21st 1928.

A glorious sunrise. The sky was a mass of tiny grey fleecy clouds – gradually they became tinged with palest rose, deepening by degrees to flaming pink Then as the sun came up they changed to purest gold, finally fading to white swansdown on a pale blue ground. Twice during the day I saw a hawk hovering over the next field - probably a Kestrel, as the Sparrow hawk does not hover over its prey. Wondered if it was after the Song Thrush, as I did not hear him singing any more after the first appearance of the hawk. Saw a jay by the ponds – and two wood pigeons flew overhead.

February 22nd

L ovely day again. birds began their chorus about 6 AM. Was relieved to see and hear the Song Thrush in his accustomed place. While I was watching him a Magpie arrived in a larch tree further up the copse, he sat there for about ten minutes, his white body gleaming in the sunshine he preened his feathers and did tail exercises, a series of jerks up and down, uttering soft caws, then five or six sharp notes in quick succession. Saw two Swans in the pond near the station In London there was a choking fog - it lifted slightly about noon. Cold night. slightly windy.

February. 23rd.

F rogs very busy in ponds, caught a large one just stepping off into the upper pond Cold and misty in the early morning - Have never seen so many birds on the shelter, there was a continual fight for a place. Put some hemp seeds on the terrace, and a chaffinch came and ate and ate - keeping all the other birds off three hen chaffinches in particular, it was most amusing to watch, while he was attacking one, another would slip in behind him, snatch a seed and make off with it. Then came a Robin and there was a battle royal, the Chaffinch being completely routed, and leaving a feather on the field.

February 25th

S aw and heard a blackbird whistling in the big Ash Tree - The Song

Thrush has not sung in the larch tree for some days. The frogs were making a tremendous noise in the ponds at noon. I thought at first it was an engine working near by. Several Hyacinths out.

February 26th

A wonderful spring day. Planted various rock plants, violets etc. worked without a coat it was so warm in the sun — Birds singing and frogs making a great noise in the two ponds. They seem to play in the upper pond, and go through the pipe to the lower one to spawn. They all came up to look at us, their grey chins just out of the water — They are a curious dull grey brown colour. pale grey under the body. They are very lively and the water is so clear now that one can see them well. Went for a walk in the woods, saw a pheasant, wood pigeons etc. Many Bees and Midges about.

February 27th

Saw two pairs of Blue Tits at the porch nest. They sat along the ariel wire just out side the window. Then the Nuthatch came and had a good look round — he seems to have abandoned the nest among the ivy as I have heard no more tapping there.

March 1st

Wake to the sound of dripping rain. Thick mist. Wrens singing in the wood very early, and a chorus of Tits Chaffinches Thrushes and Blackbirds. Watched a Song Thrush preening himself in a tree opposite. Saw several pairs of Chaffinches in the high branches, the cock kept circling round the hen, then both would fly to another branch with loud cries of "pink-pink."

March 2nd

Saw a pair of Nuthatches hunting insects on the old tree, but they paid no attention to the new nest — Tits flying about in pairs. Rain and drizzle followed by a glorious still night of moon and stars, with tiny fleecy white clouds.

March 3rd

Daffodils in flower in the garden, and several hyacinths — Scillas in full bloom. Cowslips in bud. Glorious night.

March 4th

White Violets in bloom at the gate. At Haslemere Stn saw House Sparrows collecting scraps of paper for the nests they were building under the platform bridge. They looked so draggled and dirty and one had lost most of the feathers out of his tail. Noticed the thorn bushes just breaking into green. Moon and Stars.

Woke to the sound of House Sparrows chirping and scuffling under the eaves, Moorhens calling, and wren singing. There was quite a hard frost in the night, outside my window in a pine tree a pair of sparrows were making love. being Leap year the lady was making all the advances. pursuing Mr Sparrow to the tip end of the branch! At breakfast we noticed a wren building in a nesting box on a pollarded tree, then to our astonishment we saw him building a second nest in the box on the very next tree - a few feet away. to each in turn he carried large tufts of moss, which he gathered from the foot of the trees. - Sometimes it was too large to go in comfortably, and he would give it a swing to drop it in in front of him - at other times he brought little sticks which simply wouldn't go in crossways and he got so impatient with them! We threw him out some fluffy wool - but he evidently thought us very officious, for he went away for a long time, and on his return paid no attention whatever to the wool. He was all by himself - was he building for two wives - or is he going to make a choice of houses for his bride? _ We were able to sit out all the afternoon in the sun. Birds most entertaining. At one moment there was a battle royal between a crowd of sparrows in the trees they flew at each other beating their wings and screaming - and there was a terrible hubbub.

                                          March 6th

Such a drear day, dank and drizzling. The wren has not appeared at the nests at all.. and I saw a Blue Tit inspecting one - he put his head in several times then looked round to see if anyone were noticing him - finally a great Tit chased him away, and took a look in himself.   Found Wood Anemonies in flower on a bank, and Wild Strawberries _ At 11pm heard Cock's crowing, all round the neighbourhood.

                                          March 7th

Cold drear day - Found a                  Common Daisy in bloom in the hedge. also                  Groundsel.

                                          March 8th

Starlings were very noisy                  in an elm tree near by. A pair of them came and sat in a tree                  in the garden.

**V**ery cold. some sunshine and then snow, which lay on the ground. Found Sweet Violets and a Dandelion. Saw many newborn lambs.

March 10th

**T**he day was bitterly cold. From the train saw Rooks. Crows. Swans. Wild Duck. Moorhens and Rabbits; and masses of Golden Palm.

Fernhurst.

March 11th

**S**now at intervals. some sunshine, but icy cold again. All the garden flowers have been touched by the frost. and every thing looks drear and pinched. Saw a rabbit in the lane, and found a large clump of White Violets by the outside pond. Hyacinths are out in the grass at the gate. Ponds lightly frozen over.

March 12th

**C**elandines in a garden in the village. Very cold and bleak, and snowing off and on.

March 13th

**A** wild Plum tree in full bloom near Haslemere. Snow in the morning, but soon melted away – Slightly warmer. Starlight night very still and cold.

March 14th

**V**ery thick white frost and decidedly foggy. In London there was yellow darkness till about 12.15. when the fog lifted. Starlight night.

March 16th

**M**uch warmer day. A Wren was singing wonderfully in a bush outside my window– and as soon as he had finished another one sang an answering song not far off.

March 17th

**H**eard the Nuthatch at the S wall nest– he is now a frequent visitor to the birds' tree.

March 18th 1928.

Saw a Tree Creeper on the old Plum Tree at the back gate, the first I have ever seen here. Saw and heard a Hedge Sparrow singing outside my window. The Wrens too were full of song. "Nicco" was stalking a rabbit on the green; when I shouted at him he looked round and in that moment the Rabbit darted through the hedge to safety. Frog spawn in upper ponds has hatched and there is a dense mass of wriggling blackness. Found spawn in the Lily pond and removed it.

March 19th

Rain in the night. Lilac Flowers in bud. also Ivy Leaved Speedwell. Ground Ivy in bloom

March 21st

Noticed many hairs of birds, Great Tits and Chaffinches - and on the Wagtails and Starlings. Blue Tits, March Tits Village green, Pied

March 22nd

A fat hen Pheasant was feeding outside the wood at 6.30AM. She was pecking at a piece of toast I had thrown to the chaffinches. Saw Rabbits playing at the edge of our copse - and surprised one at dusk in the lane - it ran along in front of the car for some way.

March 23rd

The garden has come on wonderfully in the last few days. Many hyacinths and grape hyacinths in full bloom. Aubretia beginning to colour. One tulip out and many others in bud. Larch trees are pale green and covered with "rosy plumelets". Thorn trees frilled with delicate green.

March 24th

Extraordinary day. Showers and a violent hailstorm in the morning, followed by a lovely afternoon and evening. Saw House Sparrows visiting the porch nest, Mr Sparrow sat on the arial wire, and Mrs Sparrow emerged from the nest with a feather in her beak. Was she stealing building material? She flew off - Then Mr Sparrow flew to the nest and clung there in a most tit-like manner looking in. Then he too, flew away. The Nuthatches have now turned their attention to the new nest on the old tree, and are doing a great deal of hammering. At Easebourne at dusk, heard Rooks cawing as they flew home to roost, Thrushes were singing, Blackbirds whistling a Wren trilling, and Ring Doves cooing.

March 25th

Fine with rather a cold wind. Cowslips in bloom. There is warfare over the porch nest. While Mrs Sparrow hops in and out of the nest. Mr Sparrow sits on the wire and keeps Mr Nuthatch away – the latter lurks in the porch waiting his opportunity to get at the nest. Hedges are getting very green, many Almond Trees are in full bloom. Also Japanese Plum. There are masses of Wood Anemones out in the copses.

March 26th

A radiantly fine day. Grass intensely green, and hedges gay with the white flowers of the thorn, and frilly green leaves which showed up vividly against the deep blue of the sky. Soft fleecy clouds chasing across the sun, and casting great shadows over the landscape. Saw Crows Nests and birds sitting, in Guildford. and Rooks near Milford. Elms are budding, and even the Oaks are very faintly tinged with pink. Sycamores are well out. Saw a Magpie up in the copse, and two Brimstone Butterflies. Mr Sparrow was at the porch nest in the morning. Roads are dusty.

March 27th

Found a Dog Violet at the edge of the wood. and Blue Bells in our copse. Saw a Wren collecting building material. Froze behind a beech and watched her go to her nest. A hole in a mud bank. She collected most of her material from close by. pieces of lichen and long dry sweet chestnut leaves. these she had some difficulty in getting in, they broke off but she always came out and fetched the broken piece from the ground. She saw me watching, but paid no attention to me, she seemed to be working entirely alone. As I stood there I heard a familiar chittering and saw a pair of long tailed Tits, one had a piece of down in its beak, so was evidently building not far away. Put out pieces of wool on the bird table, and among the ivy. Sparrows still at the porch nest.

March 28th

From the train saw clumps of Marigolds (Marsh) near Godalming.

April 1st

Very wet morning. cold bleak day. In the afternoon a very fine Cock Pheasant came into the sunk garden, and advanced towards the house, stepping high, with great dignity: suddenly he became aware of Nicco crouching at the foot of the steps. Still very dignified he turned slowly back, and went towards the low wall, one eye on Nicco all the time; he quickened his pace as the latter drew nearer, then seized with sudden panic he jumped over the wall, and as Nicco leapt after him, his dignity forsook him entirely and he ran helter skelter across the lawn and up the bank, Nicco following slowly after him. A few moments later, a second Cock Pheasant came in, with one tail feather broken and trailing, he too followed up the bank. When I went out the first bird was strolling round the ponds, then he hurried up to the copse, where his progress was stopped by the wire, instead of flying over it, he ran up and down, uttering loud cries of distress. finally he rose with a whirr and a clatter and flew down to the woods. Then I noticed the second bird up in the copse, chasing a rabbit! The latter went scuttling up the hill, the pheasant in pursuit, but the rabbit soon vanished down a burrow. Found the Wren's nest in the mud bank finished. The doorway nearly filled in with a network of twigs and leaves, and a piece of moss overhead. saw no sign of the wren. A pair of Wood Pigeons flew out of a larch tree as I passed, and high up I saw a bunch of twigs which may be their nest. A Magpie was flitting from tree to tree with harsh cries. his tail is shaped like a lance head ⟵⟋ when he flies. After tea Rabbits were playing in the     field— three large ones: They raced up and down— and round and round a little tree, then hid from each other, and jumped high in the air. There are many Dogviolets in the upper corner of the field. A few Camelias out— but most of the buds were touched by the frost last month.

April 2<sup>nd</sup> 1928.

Glorious day. Blackthorn in bloom. Found a Field Speedwell in the garden. and saw a Tree Creeper in the Village.

April 4<sup>th</sup>

The Nuthatch has won the contest for the porch nest. and is hard at work cementing the entrance. Every few minutes he arrives with a lump of mud in his beak, he is even cementing the loose bark to the box. Wild Cherry is in full bloom. Showers AM. followed by sunshine and a wonderful evening. At night a great silver moon and stars.

April 5<sup>th</sup>

Found Cuckoo flowers, or "Lady's Smock" in the garden— also Wart Cress.

April 8<sup>th</sup>

Lovely day. Sunshine, blue sky, and great billowy white clouds. Hazels are in leaf. As I was dressing I saw Martie with a baby rabbit in the garden. I thought it was dead. but just before lunch I saw it running distractedly along the path by the beech hedge. We managed to catch it, and I took it up to the copse, and put it down over the wire fence. it ran up the hill and into the first burrow. at the same moment there was a wild rush, and Mrs Rabbit appeared on the scene. Seeing me she froze— I froze— and there we remained motionless for quite fifteen minutes. Three babies emerged from the home burrow and played just outside. then I had to go. so could not see the reunion. The Nuthatch very busy all day on the porch nest. Finishing the plastering of the entrance, he cannot get it to his entire satisfaction. He gets mud from under the laurels, and applies it, then taps it into place with the tip of his beak; he works at it first from below, then from above. finally goes inside and with a sideways motion of the head smooths the plaster over with the under beak. He has made the hole so small that he can only just get out. it slants downwards like a burrow. He brought a good many dry leaves for the interior. A Peewit (Plover) flew over the Garden.

April 9th

Found a great many Wood Sorrel on the bank bordering the wood. Went up to see the Rabbits. Approached very quietly and saw one playing among the fallen leaves and another drowsing just at the entrance to the home burrow. No sign of the Wren at its nest.

April 10th

Nuthatches still very busy cementing. Mrs N has now taken the entrance in hand. Chestnut flower in bud. Every evening a bat circles round and round the front of the house.

April 12th

Heard the Cuckoo at 6.45 AM, faintly down in the valley. (It was heard in the village on the 8th) Saw Greater Stitchwort in a hedge.

April 14th

Marsh Marigolds in bloom round the ponds. Masses of cowslips. Water lilies leaves coming up. Field Wood Rush plentiful in the boggy ground round the ponds. it has long silvery hairs on its alternate leaves. Gunnera Scabra leaves opening. Still warfare over the porch nest; saw two Blue Tits stealing the leaves from inside. One had just gone inside, when up flew a second and excitedly shouted a warning into the hole, then flew off. The first instantly emerged and was gone just before the Nuthatch arrived with an angry "Tз.Tз". Cannot think what the end of it will be. Have seen the Blue Tits going in and out of the nest on the old Tree.

April 15th 1928.

Ground sprinkled with snow in the morning, and a cold wind blowing. Later it cleared and the afternoon was lovely. Found Greater Stitchwort in the lane– and White Dead Nettle—

April 16th

Thick snow lay on the ground in the morning, and it was still falling heavily. Everything in the garden was covered, not a flower to be seen anywhere. Towards noon the snow began to melt away rapidly. and by the evening when it cleared entirely there was hardly any left. A hen chaffinch ate out of C.M.S.s hand on her windowsill at 6. AM. The Blue Tits are still stealing the bedding from the Nuthatch's nest.

April 17th.

Heard the Cuckoo before 6 AM. got up and saw him sitting in a tree opposite my window. His tail goes up and his head down each time he cuckoos., a very wooden looking bird.

April 18th

Found Cuckoo Pint – and the night was starlit—

Hail fell at 7 P.M.

April 19th

Discovered a Blackbirds nest in the thicket in our field – one egg. greenish grey spotted red brown. There a good many young Blackbirds about. yellow beaks. and spotted breasts..

April 21st

A day of rain wind and sunshine. Found a Chaffinches nest in the bamboos, no eggs – and a Blackbirds nest with three young birds in it in the yew hedge. Saw a Great Tit going in and out under the eaves on the NW side of the summer house. Think there must be a Blackbirds nest in the Ivy on the E wall, as I hear one clucking there often, and I see it going in and out.

April 22nd

Found a Song Thrush's nest in a hedge in a field, the hen was sitting– the nest is in full view of everyone passing. Found another nest about 10ft up a tree, could see the tip of the hens tail. Found some curious flowers in the lane. "Horse Tail" allied to ferns. jointed stems, and rigid leaves in circles at the joints. Went to see the Blackbirds nest in the thicket. and found an egg hatching

April 23rd

Went for a walk on Blackdown. Woods carpeted with Wood Anemones.

Wood Sorrel. Dog Violets etc. In one field primroses were growing in great cushions, and the ground was covered with Ground Ivy, in full bloom. Also Dog Violets. Here I found pink Campion and Moschatel with its' head of five green flowers four back to back, topped by the fifth. Found fourteen nests during the day. Some were too high to see into. Hedge Sparrow sitting in a low hedge. Eggs a lovely blue. A Blackbirds nest had four babies in it. A Robins nest was beautifully built into a hole about ten feet up a tree. Eggs white shaded and speckled with pinky red. A Blackbirds nest in a holly tree on the hill. Eggs greenish blue, speckled and mottled brown. Another Blackbirds nest was high in a holly tree by the side of the road. A Song Thrush's nest in a conspicuous place in the wood, the bird sitting on four lovely blue eggs, speckled black. One Chaffinch's nest, beautifully made of moss and softly lined with hair and feathers, had been torn out. A Tits nest I think - a tiny moss one, high in a slender tree.

April 25th

Saw a Swan sitting on its nest, near Godalming. In the early morning two Cuckoos were making love in the big Ash tree. It was a very close warm day.

April 26th

For the first time, I heard a Black Cap singing, and looking up saw it sitting in the topmost branch of a Sallow. The Blackcap migrates in winter, returning in late March, or in April. The Woods are full of Wood Sanicle coming into flower. Found several old nests, and one new - a Chaffinches - but no eggs in it. Passed The Song Thrush sitting tight in her conspicuous nest in the field. was careful not to disturb her. In Midhurst I saw a Peacock Butterfly, and a Small White - Rooks were cawing loudly round their nest. I saw a Wren hopping along the opposite bank of a stream, then disappear behind a stump. I think it must have had a nest there. A very warm day with brilliant sunshine.

April 27th.

Lilac in flower in the village. and Laurel here is in full bloom. Wistaria out in patches. At dusk saw a fine Cock Pheasant accompanied by two hens in the wood, and heard a Wren singing almost incessantly in the big holly tree. I feel sure he has a nest in the Travellers Joy which grows in a tangle all over the top of the tree. Saw a Queen Wasp on the Ivy on my E wall.

April 28th

A marvellous day. glowing sunshine, and quite hot.

April 29th

Some of our lilac out. Bugle in full bloom. Dandelions terribly abundant.

May 1st 1928.

**G**rey early. warm sunshine later. The rain of the 29th (night) has brought on the trees wonderfully, and the oaks are now a glorious golden green, or bronze. "Oak before Ash, splash splash, splash": no sign of Ash as yet, Beech hedge is growing green.— Found Germander Speedwell fully out.

May 3rd

**F**ound "Pig Nut" in the wood, and in the lane Yellow Dead Nettle. and Common Speedwell (with lilac flowers) also 3 Nerved Sandwort, which has 3 distinct veins up the back of each leaf.—

May 5th

**G**lorious Summers day very warm. On Blackdown found a beautiful Tiger Beetle scurrying among the heather, a bright green fellow with yellow spots. Found White and also blue Milkwort — The woods were full of bracken, its fronds still curled. Bluebells. etc — found a white bluebell, and Tormentil. Cow Parsley in all the hedges. and "Jack-in-the Hedge."

May 6th

**F**ound Forget-me-not and Crosswort Bedstraw in the lane.

May 7th

**H**op Trefoil in the field. Crane Flies, or Daddy Longlegs are everywhere. if one opens a cupboard or touches a box, a Crane fly leaps up in ones face. Mosquitos too are very active. Fields are yellow with meadow buttercups. Was shown a Robin's nest with young just hatching, in a bank. cunningly concealed in a hole among the grass. Also a nest of young Thrush.

May 9th

**V**ery cold and windy. In the lower fields saw many young thrushes feeding on the ground, some being fed by the parents, The Song Thrush in her conspicuous nest in the field, has hatched out her babies safely. and the growing leaves now hide them from prying eyes. Common Purple or Red Clover in the garden. and in the fields Common Purple Orchids.

May 10th

**A**gain cold, but very fine — cloudy towards evening — Found Yellow Pimpernel in the lane. Heard a great deal of twittering and fluttering outside my window, and there were The Spotted Flycatchers — sitting on the telephone wires, and on the edge of the roof. One flashed past my head in pursuit of a fly — They seemed to be hunting for a nesting site. Found a White Ermine moth on the terrace. brought it in to the house. but it had evidently been chilled. and soon died.

**T**he Song Thrush babies in the field have flown. Found Bulbous Buttercup in the field, a short stalk, and the Sepals folded back against it — also found "Upright Crowfoot" or Meadow Buttercup a tall variety with sepals spread under the petals —
Thought I heard Nightingales far down in the Valley.

**S**aw a Great Tit going in and out of a large crevis. in the wall where it evidently has a nest with young, but too far in for anyone to see. Our watching it did not seem to worry the Tit in the least — he came and went about every three minutes —

**W**hile gardening found all kinds of strange things among the roots of plants — centipedes. grubs etc — and one lovely little crimson spider, about three times the size of a "money spider" The Spotted Flycatchers very busy round the house. their chirp is a loud insistant ss .ss. ss. and sit swaying on the telephone wires, looking at me with the greatest unconcern, Then suddenly darting swiftly in pursuit of a fly. H.T.S. killed a Queen Wasp in the drawingroom, the fourth I have seen this year — Pale pink May nearly in full bloom. Ash trees growing green.

**L**ooking out of my window, I saw a baby Robin ,contemplating a large wriggling worm, not at all knowing how to tackle it. (he had more the appearance of a very small Thrush being rather mottled, and with brown spots on a light breast. young Robins do not get their red waiscoats before the autumn.) One of his parents soon joined him, and whisking up the worm, led the baby off to the shelter of the lilac bushes. The Great Tit was making regular journeys to and fro, feeding his young. The Nuthatch babies are not yet big enough to feed themselves I imagine, as he flies to the nest, and passes the food to Mrs N, not going in himself at all. Thunder and a little rain in the afternoon — Sunshine in the evening. Found Common Fumitory in the back garden.

**R**escued a baby rabbit from Martie, and put it back in a burrow in our copse, am rather afraid it may have come from the woods, but can only hope it was kindly received. Found Common Avens or "Herb Bennet" in the village; and Ragged Robin by our Upper Pond.

**A** bitterly cold day, windy and raining, though the sun shone at intervals. From the train, going to Newhaven, the country was beautiful — hedges white with May. and Cow Parsley. fields yellow with Buttercups. and on the banks were quantities of Campions (pink) Saw six Swans in the Harbour. They swam slowly out to meet the incoming boat.

May 17th 1928.

A fine morning, and heavy thundershowers in the afternoon.

May 18th

Very wet day followed by a starlight night. Found Black Medick at Midhurst. After tea when the rain had ceased, watched three rabbits at play in the field – They were very busy shaking the wet off their paws, and cleaning their faces – The Nuthatches are feeding their young on pieces of snail, and green Caterpillars.

May 19th

Found Dove's Foot Crane's Bill in the wild garden and met a young frog which hopped almost under my feet. A Dingey Skipper Butterfly was sunning itself on some Hop Trefoil. I went to look at the Chaffinch's nest in the bamboos and to my surprise found the hen sitting – I think she must be our "Tame". for she never moved though I was within two feet of her. I crept away again so as not to disturb her. In the afternoon there was a tremendous storm, with thunder, lightening, hail and rain. Saw Oak Apples on the trees on Friday Hill.

May 20th

In the lane I found Black Bryony – Thrushes and Blackbirds were singing. Up in our Copse I saw Rabbits at play. and heard Blackbirds calling their young among the bushes. A Robin accompanied me, hopping from tree to tree, singing his joyous little song. The Nuthatches are very busy, making their entrance smaller, I imagine in order to keep the young in, I saw beaks stretching up! Mr N uses the mud from the outside, in the bark, for this purpose. He was working hard at it for a long time. Mrs N spends most of her time inside with the babies.

May 21st

Great Tit is still feeding its young in the wall nest. Saw a pair of Blackbirds at the Shelter – Mr B sat in an apple Tree while Mrs B with great difficulty collected two large pieces of bread in her beak, then off they both flew to the copse – Where they had evidently left their babies. Saw a pair of Spotted Flycatchers in the orchard.

May 23rd

Saw a flock of Martins circling round and round over a field near Haslemere. the first I have chanced to see this year. A very dull wet day. The Pigeon at Westminster were sitting dejectedly in little huddled heaps in an enclosed green near the Abbey.

May 25th

A glorious day. Many butterflies sunning themselves on the flowers.

large white and many small white. Resued two little White-
Pinion Spotted Moths from the lily pond, and placed
them in the sun to dry. They soon recovered com- pletely.
They are pure creamy white with two triangular black spots
at the edge of each front wing. — A small dragonfly was
hovering over the pond. the second I have seen this year. Saw
two Grizzled Skippers on one flower, and near by a Dingey Skipper.
The Great Tit and the Nuthatch are still busy feeding their young.
Found Hairy Vetch, very narrow leaved and tangley, with minute
white flowers. In the Village saw a House Martin's nest under eaves.

May 26<sup>th</sup>

Robin has a lovely little nest in one of the rockery walls in a
creviss and under the shelter of an overhanging plant. I can
just see mrs Rs bright beady eyes and red gills over the edge of the
nest. Saw Blue Tits feeding their young in a nest under the corner of the roof. (N.E.) A Kestrel was hovering over the fields and
wood for a long time — At times he seemed to be absolutely
stationary, for ten and even twelve seconds without so much
as an apparent wing beat — I wonder if he has a
nest any where near, as I frequently see him over the
fields. Kestrels build in old ruins, or very hight trees,
sometimes in other birds vacated nests. They are
easily dis- tinguished from the Sparrow Hawk which
never hovers but darts straight down on its prey.
Saw two pairs of Doves by the potting
sheds. These I think must be Stock
Doves. They evidently have nests near
by. as they are always about. Found two
curious little insects on the briar hedge — something between a beetle and a bee.

May 27<sup>th</sup>

Puck brought in a large baby rabbit at breakfast, and was promptly chased
and made to disgorge. The rabbit bounded off up the steps into the orchard
where I found it later, caught it, and put it over the wire — it ran up to
the wood where I hope it found its home. Found a Large
Red-Belted Clearwing Moth in the diningroom window, and later,
while planting out anthirrinums, came across a fat Cockchafer, lying
helpless on its back. Put it on its feet, and it crawled laboriously about
on the low wall, finally vanished. The Cockchafer is hatched in the
autumn, and as a grub lives for four years in the ground, eating veg-
etables — when it leaves the pupal stage it sleeps for six or seven months
before emerging as a full blown insect. It then lives on trees —
Oak and elm principally. and they themselves are the prey of
many birds, pigs, bats, and even cats! Watched the pond skaters on the

Lily pond. There are three large fat Tadpoles in the pond, think They must be Natterjack Toad Tadpoles, as it is late for frogs. Three lovely red bodied Dragon flies were hovering over the pink tinted lily leaves, They are smaller and more delicate than the irridescent green ones. After dinner There was a terrible commotion among the Robins in the wood. I ran down and found two parent robins chattering and scolding Martie, who was evidently hunting for their nest. I chased him away, but it was a long time before the alarm subsided. Strata clouds were sweeping across the sky in the morning, and the night was windy.

May 28th 1928.

The Great Tits have evidently flown safely. I think I saw one of them on the wall this morning. Foxgloves are in bloom. Warm day and very fine. The Nuthatches have been very busy filling in all the slits in the nest with mud, even working on the top, and up the side of the porch behind the nest. They peck the surface of the wood until it is picked up like wool, then they mix mud with bark on the old tree and apply it. The babies make a great noise at times.

May 29th

Warmer still, the air rather thundery. Cloudy towards evening with wind rising. One Yellow Flag out in the lower ponds. and a Common Blue Butterfly fluttering on the bank. Almost stepped on a baby toad. Saw many small Heath Butterflies in the field and a Green Veined White. Found Bird's foot Trefoil and Yellow Pimpernel. or Wood Loosetrife. also Ivy-Leaved Toadflax. (Linaria) Coming home in the car, met a Cock and a hen pheasant in the lane. They do not mind the car in the least, and will let it come quite close up to them, so long as they do not see the people in it.

May 30th.

Found a queer little flying beetle in the garden. black with red markings. Dog Roses in bloom. Painted Lady Butterfly at Fernden.

May 31st

Came across one of the baby Great Tits. dead on the terrace. The work of one of the cats I am afraid. Very windy day, but no rain. ground getting very dry.

June 1st

Young Nuthatches have not yet flown. and no sign of them looking out at the entrance. Found White Evening Campion in the field, and Common Sow. or Milk Thistle. also Rough Hawkbit. Saw many Small Heath Butterflies Very windy. S Easterly. Bright moonlight and stars.

June 2nd.

The Nuthatches had not left the nest, when we left at 4.30 pm. nor were They looking out, so this year They are later than last as They flew on the 2nd. I expect the delay is owing to the competition for the nest. Heavenly day, though very windy.

# France.

### Havre                    to                    Caen.

Flowers more advanced than at home. Masses of Yellow Flag Iris in the
marshes. and Common Reed by the wayside.  Crows seemed to have their
nests in the high chalk cliffs. I saw them resting on the ledges, and going
into the holes. Stinging nettles in flower and I think I saw Greater Willow
Herb.— At Quillebœuf watched a swallow skimming backwards and forwards
over the water, always over the same spot, his back gleaming a wonderful deep
sapphire blue in the sunshine, then suddenly he rose in the air and crossed the
river, followed by his mate.— Later in the day I saw many Swifts. They are
larger than Swallows— and a dark sooty brown, their wings very
long and curved, so that when flying they
are shaped exactly like a drawn bow. As we
drove along I heard the familiar songs of the
Wrens Chaffinches and thrushes.    Jackdaws were
nesting in the oblong openings in the towers of
the Eglise de la Trinité at Caen— also Swallows
a Glorious day— and very warm— but it
grew cooler towards evening— Swifts flew
constantly over the courtyard where we sat. uttering shrill yet musical cries.

### Caen                    to                    Rennes.

In the fields saw many Oxeye Daisies and Common Red Poppies. and in the
hedges Tamarisk, Foxgloves, and Pink and White Campions.  Saw a Yellow
Hammer., and several Magpies. At Mont St Michel there were hundreds
of Cockchafers lying dead and dying on the castle steps. I only saw one
on the wing Swallows were nesting in the chimneys. and many Swifts
flying about.— Saw spotted Orchis.—

### Rennes                    to                    Saintes.

Country very flat and rather uninteresting, but the hedges full of wild
flowers Profusion of Dog Roses and fragrant Honeysuckle. Privet is
also out, and we passed under avenues of delicate scented Accacias in
bloom. White Water Lillies were out on many of the ponds, and all along
the roadside White Dutch Clover was growing. Many fields were white with
Oxeye Daisies sprinkled with Poppies and Field Scabious I also saw Cam-
panulas and Tufted Vetch. also Scotch Thistles.   In many places the hay was
cut, and wheat already in the ear.   The Magpie is a very common bird
here, every few minutes one sees one cross the road flying low. and they
seem very tame, for one sees them in the village streets and gardens, pecking about almost like hens.   They go about in pairs and I saw two
sitting face to face on a branch in a low tree.  Vines are about
eighteen inches high.— I saw Valerian growing on a rocky bank— and
Hemlock Storks Bill on a stone wall.

Santes to Bordeaux.                    June 6th 1928.

Saw Quaking Grass - and Blackberry in flower. Stonecrop growing on roofs.
Teasles in the hedges. Passed the first Umbrella Pine I have seen this trip.
Hedge Bedstraw in profusion on the banks. Scotch Thistles. Did not see a single
Magpie, so we are evidently out of their country. Oxen are used here for everything,
ploughing, mowing, and hauling hay; they move very slowly and heavily and
wear coarse string veils over their faces, to keep off the flies. Saw fields of
oats in the ear. and Meadow Sage by the roadside.

                    Bordeau to St Jean de Luz.              June 7th

Passed through miles of Pine forests. nearly every tree     being tapped for
its turpentine. A large slice is cut downwards off the bark.   well into the wood.
a curved strip of tin nailed across the bottom to catch       the oozing lumps
which looks rather like yellow drippings. it then             runs into a
cone shaped earthenware receptacle -        We also          saw miles
of Cork Trees. avenues of them, denuded of         their   bark to a
height of 6 or 7 feet-              - the bare part being a dark sooty
brown.                            Soil very soft and peaty. Found
Bell                              Heather and Yarrow. Grass and
Heather                           were growing under the pines,
and                               sheep were being pastured there.
In other                          parts bracken was growing
knee            high.   The              "tapping" does not seem
to improve the pines, as they            looked very unhealthy all
the lower branches dead. and the         upper ones        very brown.
Saw two Greater Spotted Woodpeckers    fly across the       road.
very handsome birds. I also saw the first House Martin I have      seen
in France.   Yellow Rock Roses in masses. Our road
was bordered by Planes for miles & miles.  No oxen            used
in this district, but Mules with wonderful trappings.
                                        June 8th
            St Jean de Luz - to - Oloron.
Very hot and thundery. Saw four magpies and a Jay. This
is again a district of Oxen. They are always harnessed in pairs
their heads yoked together with a strip of wood, bound to their huge
horns, and covered with shaggy white fur to keep the sun off.
They also wear blankets of white cotton with a coloured border, to
keep off the flies which are very bad. Saw Verbascum
or Great Mullein in full bloom. also Scarlet Pimpernel, Everlasting
Pea (Narrow leaved) and many spotted orchids.   Found ripe
wild Strawberries and whilst picking them saw two Lizards dart
into holes in the rocks- Saw a very large bird hovering and wheeling
then a crow darted out and gave chase. and they flew higher and higher,       the
crow seemed to be attacking the larger bird which was about three times his
size - Asked a passer-by what it was, and he said a kind of Vulture- and that

it stole baby chicks. Its wings were barred dark brown. and it had a wide fan shaped tail with which it seemed to steer, by slanting it sideways. Saw another bird like it very soon afterwards. Saw two lovely little black and yellow birds about the size of a chaffinch. they were on the wing, so I could not see them very well. The walls at Oloron were covered with Ivy Leaved Toadflax. and Maidenhair Spleenwort. there was also a good deal of Spotted Dead Nettle. In places the ground was carpeted with Tormentil.

June 9th

### Oloron-to- Bagnères de Luchon.

Very hot. day, scorching sun. Beautiful scenery. Snow Capped Pyrenees and verdant foothills. Saw many flowers I could not name. A tall thick straight stem with a poker top of starry white or very pale lilac flowers springing from a group of blade like leaves- like our garden Tritoma - then a very pretty little deep red purple flower with leaves like common Avens. - Beautiful blue starry flowers like upright Campanulas Saw a great deal of Doves-foot Cranes Bill. but with bright pink flowers. Snakeweed in the fields, and very pink Scabious. Brookline by a stream. At the top of the Col de Payresoude I found Common Comfrey - Variegated Coronilla. and Tuberous Saxifrage (Pretty Maids) also Viola- exactly like our garden Viola Cornuta By the roadside I saw a group of lovely large Yellow Poppies, as big as Shirley Poppies. Also Musk, or Nodding Thistle, and Bladder Campion. The slopes of the mountains in parts were white with Narcissi. Lizards kept darting across the road, and among the rocks, moving incredibly swiftly. Saw House Martins at their mud nests under eaves.

June 11th

### Bagnères de luchon to Foix.

A grey day and almost cold. Saw Slender leaved Flax (lilac flower) and Yellow Rattle. Heard the Cuckoo for the first time since we came over, and saw many Magpies. A big glittering bronze beetle fell into the car. it flew out when I opened the door. At Foix I found in the castle grounds Greater Broom -rape- Vipers Bugloss, and Wallrue Spleenwort. and two Vetches I could not name one with mauve and the other with blue flowers. Also a tall plant about 15 in high growing in the walls. covered with tiny greeny pinky bells -

### FOIX TO PERPIGNAN.

June 12th

Fields golden with Yellow Rattle. Many Pyramidal Orchis by the road side, pale and deep pink. and very large. Saw one Cuckoo and heard another. Many Cypress trees, mostly in church yards. Saw Meadow Vetchling (yellow) and Carthusian's Pink. Campanulas with enormous bells. (as big as garden Canterbury's) and large mauve stars on slender stems, about 12 in high. The roadside was carpeted in places with lesser Bindweed - some white some pink. much larger than ours at home. I never saw anything like the masses of honeysuckle, all in full bloom. some a rich deep pink and some golden yellow it's fragrance filled the air, also that of the yellow sweet scented broom, which grows in great profusion down here. We passed along a road where for about ½ mile the fir trees were covered with enormous cocoons. some of which looked almost like wasps nests. We came upon a fascinating tiny Owl about 8 or 9 inches high, sitting on a low wall - he flew into a tree, and sitting on a small bough he peeped at us over another his great eyes wide with surprise, then as we backed to get a better view of him he flew away. I saw another Great Spotted Woodpecker - Olive Trees - and prickley spikey leaved.Cactus - Saw our Saponaria Gcymoides growing wild in masses. Large bushes of pink Rock Roses - and a very pretty pale sulpher yellow Dandelion. with thick fleshy leaves, stalks and buds.

June 15th 1928

### Perpignan to St Baynuls to Perpignan.

Wonderful deep rose pink convolvulus by the roadside., the flowers shaped like Greater Bindweed - but the leaves more like Scented Geranium and small high - with leaved Woodpecker. the road.
They were twined round tall grasses shrubs. Gigantic Thistles about 3½ feet great purple heads. Fleshy round Cactus - Saw another Great Spotted also a large snake wriggling across

June 14th

### Perpignan to Carcassonne.

Common Flax, and some small plants of Chicory. Saw Masses sweet scented I saw growing our garden Common and more like oats
of Spotted Dead Nettle. and all along the road Yellow Broom filled the air with its fragrance in the hedges large Everlasting Pea - like kind. Found creeping Cinquefoil and Centaurea - also Rest Harrow, but a taller bushy kind than ours. Grasses all along the road, and in the hedges.

I found some very pretty little flowers like Lesser Bindweed. but on an upright stem, with narrow leaves. Also clumps of little yellow button flowers about 9in high. silvery stems, and with a strong aromatic scent. Also a flower like Knapweed with stiff prickles all over the Calyx Saw a Jay - and in the old Cité of Carcassonne fas- cinating little yellow Lizards, covered with tiny dark shell

(santolina)

### Carcassonne.

**V**ery windd, and the air full of dust. Rather a grey morning – The waste ground in the Old Cité is covered with Common Mallow.

### Carcassonne to Albi.

**G**lorious scenery, Mountains and valleys – slopes yellow with Common Broom – with occasional patches of the sweet scented. There were carpets of Creeping Thyme by the roadside, and I saw a very pretty, blue flower almost like a large daisy. The Thistles were Carmine-mauve, a marshy spot was covered with cotton grass, and orchis, and I saw a whole field of red sorrel, which at the first glance looked like poppies, it was such an intense red. One field was a picture, with poppies in a carpet of some purple flower. I found Bee Orchis, and yet another kind of upright Convolvulus. Saw Meadow Sweet in the hedges and Yellow Bedstraw. Many golden Rock Roses, and a very tiny Slender Leaved Flax, palest blue flowers. We came through a 20 kilometre avenue of beautiful tall plane Trees. interlaced overhead. Saw a Dove and a little Owl, a Jay and many pairs of Magpies.

### Albi to Tulle.

**M**arvellously extensive views on all sides – roads running along high ridges, and winding along wooded slopes and through green valleys. Mountains in the distance a rich deep blue. Glimpsed a Green Woodpecker, and also a Nuthatch which was sitting on a gate – Jays and many Magpies – at one moment I saw five of them all together in the road. they give long laborious hops before they rise into the air, and balance themselves with an upward jerk of the tail when they alight – Carpets of Thyme by the wayside. At Tulle there were many fish in the river – from 12 to 14 inches long. Watched the Swallows skimming over the water and under the bridges – and on the opposite side a Grey Wagtail was watching for flies, sitting on a jutting spike in the wall., every now and then he made a dart at the surface of the water, then returned to his post of vantage. Just over our windows on the balcony House Martins had their nests. Tulle was the only place where I saw Swifts Swallows and Martins.

### Tulle to Chateauroux.

**S**aw a large bright green Lizard dart across the road. They move incredibly fast! Many Magpies and Jays – and today I saw three Green Wood-peckers, on the pecker. the second one settled, and I saw him well, clinging to the side of a tree – the first one I have ever been able to see properly. More avenues of Maples, and some of Beech. I have not seen many of the latter in France – in any case they do not lend themselves to being trimmed, as their whole beauty lies in their lower spreading Branches. Saw many eating Chest-nut trees – there seemed to be forests of them.

**June 19th 1928.**

## Chateauroux to Chartres.

Rather flat uninteresting country after the hills and mountains. Very few vines - but acres and acres of potatoes. The fields of cultivated clover are lovely, and here and there among the deep crimson are vivid patches of vermillion poppies. We passed a small field of white Dutch Clover, which was deliciously fragrant. The fields of green wheat were tinged with the glorious sapphire blue of the Cornflowers, and there were golden acres of mustard. Saw a Sparrow hawk - a Dove - and many Yellow Hammers.

**June 20th**

## Chartres to Caudebec.

Saw Apple Trees still in full bloom, while a cherry tree was covered with ripe red cherries! Saw many Yellow Hammers, a Green Woodpecker, and a flock of Starlings. Magpies in plenty, some of them were following the plough. Hay was being cut, and one field of Barley, cut and stooked. Saw Corn Cockle, and all the crops were full of Cornflowers and Poppies. ~~ A great many Musk Thistles, and Sainfoin (Cocks Head) also Meadow Sage. Heard Larks singing, and saw them soaring high overhead.

**June 21st**

## Caudebec -

On the way to Jumièges, saw some very pretty crops of mixed red and white clover, and among them were growing poppies, Cornflowers and Mustard. In the wheat were the most beautiful CornCockles, about 3½ feet high, with many spreading branches. Watched House Martins building their nests under some eaves - some had nearly finished, one had half done the inside, and was moulding with his breast. Others were only just beginning. It seems late for them to be building, as at home the nests were finished three weeks ago.

**June 22nd**

## Caudebec to Havre

A lovely day, and very pretty country. The Poppies among the corn and cultivated clover glowed vividly red in the sunshine. Hayfields full of pink grasses and Oxeye Daisies. Marigolds growing in the corn. There were many Jackdaws wheeling and hovering round the cliffs, their grey heads gleaming silver in the Sunlight. They evidently had nests in the holes in the cliffs, they sat in rows on the ledges - Saw Martins there and their mud nests under the overhanging ridges. Up by the Hève Lighthouses nearly trod on a wonderful bronze and green beetle with gold stripes down his back, and red legs.

**June 23rd**

## England.

On our way from Southampton to Fernhurst noticed how thick the foliage has become during our Three works absence. Many less flowers in the hedges. and by the wayside, Than in France. Saw a baby Rabbit. Wrens and Chaffinches singing loudly— Jays now come on The birds shelter — and make a great noise in the surrounding Trees.

June 24th

The garden is full of colour. Oriental Poppies, Anchusas, Delphineius Lupins Canterbury Bells, Pinks etc. The ground is very dry, and seedlings are stunted for want of rain. Saw a Chiff Chaff for the first time in my life -he was hop- ping about on the top of the fruit cage. and on the pea sticks. The Chaffinches are extraordinarily tame, and come in at the dining room door, to pick up Polly's seed. from the floor, They also hop about the window sills asking for the windows to be opened — The upper ponds are full of Water Bedstraw. In the lane found Water Forget-me-not. Hedge Parsley. Small Flowered Hairy Willow Herb. Hedge Woundwort. and Lesser Stitchwort. White Plume Thistle.

June 25th

G.M.S called me to her room at 8.30AM as our pet Chaffinch "Brave" had been eating from her hand. I tried and he came again and again. First I held the bread between my fingers, each time he took it and flew away to a Sycamore to hide it, or eat it. Then I put the crumbs on the palm of my hand, and he came just the same, again and again. and sometimes stayed to eat the crumbs on the sill. He pecked my fingers quite hard! at breakfast he kept coming in, and picking up the crumbs we threw him. I was in the drawing room when I heard a great cheeping going on out- side. Looked out and saw a great fat baby Cuckoo sitting on the top of the finest cage. being fed by a small bird who was standing on tiptoe. pushing food down his throat. The little bird then went off to get more. and The cuckoo continued to sit in a fat lump, keeping up an incessant cry for food, with his very red mouth wide open. Then something startled him and he flew away down to the woods. At 4 o'c I heard his cry again and saw him fly across the orchard to a tree in the field. the little bird was very busy feeding him, hunting among the bracken, and stuffing the lazy fat thing every two or three minutes. Could not distin- guish what the little bird was, but it looked very like a white throat. At about 8.30 saw the young Cuckoo going to roost in the copse—follow- ed by his foster mother.

June. 26th

Complete change of weather Wind and rain in gusts, towards evening it cleared a little. Saw about six Starlings on the lawn, very busy picking about. Surprised a rabbit in the upper field. Found Self Heal, and Meadow Vetchling (yellow) Nipplewort, and Wall Lettuce. Lesser Spearwort in the ponds.

June 27th 1928

Fine day again - rather cold early. Found Hairy Hawkbit, single flower on about 12 to 14 in stem. All the leaves from the root, the calyx very hairy - Long rooted Cat'sear - long branched flower stalks, leaves from the root. In the lane found Wall Lettuce, and Nipplewort - Marsh Ragwort in the pond outside - Rose Bay, of the Willow Herb tribe. Again saw starlings in the garden.

June 30th

Sunny morning. Tremendous showers in the afternoon. Again saw the young Cuckoo being fed, first he was on the fruit cage, then he flew away to a post and sat there for ages. His foster-mother was very busy hunting food for him among the cabbages, then on a birch tree - to feed him, she ran up his back, and he turned his head over his shoulder, with his wide red mouth open to receive the food which she then popped in, and flew off for more. He kept up an incessant cry for food. It must be exhausting work for the foster mother, feeding such a large bird, and she soon led him off to roost in the copse. About an hour later he was back again - sitting very dejected - and crying, but no foster mother came.

July 1st

Early, I heard a curious unfamiliar bird call outside my window. A harsh sound, between a "chip" and a "chuck" often repeated. But I could see nothing. A little later I saw in the drawing room, and heard it again - looking out I saw a Great Spotted Woodpecker, climbing up the birdshelter - All day at intervals he came, now on the apple trees, hunting insects, now on the shelter, pecking at the basket of fat. Most fascinating to watch. He worked always upwards, circling round the tree, disappearing and reappearing - The Jays are continually in the orchard and on the shelter - one stands in the saucer of water, and stretches up to the bag of fat, taking occasional little leaps at it, while another sits at the corner crying to be fed by one of the parents. There seem to be two young ones and a parent always together - They hop about in the long grass, searching for food - they like bread, and swallow large cubes of it. Saw a young Blackbird being fed at the back door by its mother - Saw two Missel Thrush, the first I have seen since the winter. Found Goutweed - or Ground Elder in flower - I weeded out some grass from a step, and out fell a gigantic worm - almost instantly it coiled up like a spring, and actually jumped back into the hole and vanished. In the evening I saw the young cuckoo on a post all alone - I think the foster parents must have at last turned it off to find its own food. He flew away into the field

July 2nd

Tied a walnut to one of the apple trees, a small piece cracked out of it. Saw no bird on it each time I looked out. But most

of the kernel was gone by the evening. Saw several Thrush.
There was a tremendous commotion among a party of Great
Tits before breakfast. discovered Martie stalking them, and
called him off.

July 3rd

Rather a dull day, and rain in the evening - Again saw the Great
Spotted Woodpecker in the orchard. it is the fat he comes for.
He is very shy, and flies off if he hears anyone near. I think the
Great Tits must be raising a second brood in the nest in the wall
I heard a great cheeping and chirping in there as I passed by.
no Tit came while I watched - Later in the evening I saw a
Blackbird fly out from that direction with a great clatter, but
I do not think it could be his nest. Martie hears the twittering
and lies on the top of the wall listening -

July 4th

As I passed near the Great Tits' old nest in the wall, I heard a great twittering
and chittering, which ceased directly I stood in front of the hole; when I
moved away it began again - Later I saw the Tit going to the nest with food.

June 5th

In Midhurst I found Upright Yellow Wood Sorrel and Silver Weed. The edge
of the Lake was covered with Lesser Duckweed. In the afternoon
the Great Spotted Woodpecker came to the shelter, bringing his young daughter,
(She has no red on the nape of the neck, and her underbody is fainter in
colouring. She sat in an appletree while he fetched lumps of fat with
which he fed her, also bits of walnut which I had wedged in below the
fat - They remained for quite an hour, and were most amusing to
watch. When they fly their red underbodies show very distinctly - Saw
a kestrel hovering - and he was joined by another - The jays continues
to be very noisy.

June 6th

Found Woody or Bitter-
in Fernhurst, also Fig-
on the wing - The Great
about from time to time - but
young Cuckoo has quite
Tit is still feeding his babies
early morning saw two rabbits on
my E. Window., a large one and a
covered me suddenly, and stamped
froze. The baby heard no atten-
time the big one went on
road startled him, and
followed by the baby.

sweet Nightshade
Saw a Goldfinch
Woodpecker was
no baby. The
ished. The Great
the wall. In the
"The green" outside
baby. The former dis-
loudly to warn the baby, then
tion whatever, and after a
feeding till something up the
stamping wildly he fled

wort.
Spotted
I saw
van-
in

June 7th

Great Spotted Woodpecker
came, but was more
audacious, coming close

about, and the baby also
independent. The jays are most
to the diningroom door to be fed

and quarrelling loudly in the Holly Tree. The young ones who are every bit as big as their parents, clamour for food, and look too absurd hopping after their parents, squealing and opening wide their beaks. The Great Tit is still feeding his family. He alights on a nearby rose tree and peers cautiously about to see that no one is looking _ and if he catches sight of me, he flies up into the holly tree and waits.

July 8th

The young Great Spotted Woodpecker is beginning to be quite on her own. Her father brought her to the orchard and left her _ she soon got hungry and decided to try the shelter. First she sat on the table - then went underneath and had a good peck at the walnuts, then the fat - this she got at from all angles. She was there for ages - then Mr G. S. Woodpecker joined her, and they flew off together. Water lillies are blooming in the upper pool, from two roots which I threw in last autumn, from the lily pond. The surface of the upper pond is covered with thick green slime

July 9th

The Great Spotted Woodpecker baby came by herself to the shelter, and had a tremendous feed of fat, the basket had been replenished. She attacked it from all sides, and finally sat on top of it _ She and Mr G. S. W were about in the big Ash tree a great deal, and I kept hearing their harsh call. At tea time "Brave" (Chaffinch) came in at the door repeatedly for crumbs which I threw him. By the fruit cage on the pea sticks I saw a Whitethroat. and I think a Willow Warbler a slender little bird, very yellow about the throat and underbody _ Found Common Enchanters Nightshade in the wood and Square Stemmed St John's Wort in the lane. Leaning from my E window at 11pm heard frogs singing down in the valley_

July 10th

A wonderful day of warmth and sunshine "Brave" came in for crumbs at breakfast. _ the G. S. Woodpeckers were about. Baby Chaffinches were being fed on the shelter, and a big fat baby Jay. A Flycatcher (Spotted) comes to the window and flutters there in an upper corner, probably catching flies _ Saw a Plover sailing overhead, uttering his plaintive pee-weet_ Many Meadow Brown Butterflies. Martie had a baby rabbit, and carried it off before I could save it.

July 11th

Great Spotted Woodpeckers were making a tremendous noise in the oak tree opposite my E window in the morning, calling repeatedly, but the foliage is so thick I could not see them. Saw a Swift flying low in the churchyard _ Nicco stalked a young Jay in the Orchard, but I just frightened it away in time.

July 12th

A very hot day. blazing sunshine and very little breeze. At dinner

"Brave" came in, but I had to put crumbs out on the terrace for him. as Puck was in the room.

July 14th

Hotter still. and altogether heavenly weather. Cloudless blue sky. Gentle sea breeze at Bognor. On the way saw Yellow Water Lillies at Midhurst, in the hedges Greater and Lesser Bindweed. Great Hairy Willow Herb, and Field Scabious. also Musk Mallow. Saw a Wood Pigeon in a field. also a Plover. Masses of Rose Bay on a slope, glowing vivid pink against a deep blue sky. Golden fields of Mustard. and crops of wheat, and ripening oats. Sparkling blue sea with tiny plashing waves. After dusk a still heavy night.

July 15th

An intensely hot day; at 5PM unable to endure the heat we went and sat in front of the Summer House in the shade. There was a faint breeze which grew gradually fresher as the sun sank lower. A cloudless sky, and a marvellously clear view of the downs and Chanctonberry Ring. A Wood pigeon flew over and a Great Spotted Woodpecker was busy tapping high up on a rotten bough. The song of the birds was hushed for it was too hot I think even for them and plants are shrivelling in the burning sun. Suddenly a field Mouse dashed across the end of the path, and two seconds later a Stoat followed. Ran down, but both had completely disappeared. Found Climbing Persicaria or Convolvulus Knotgrass. a Dahlia is in flower. I was pulling up old plants of oxeye daisies in the crazy pavement, and disturbed a colony of Brown Garden Ants nesting under a root. They came out in swarms. The non-workers were winged, and I noticed one which was quite twice the size of all the others. There seemed to be no eggs being carried about.

+ July 17th

In the garden found Common Centauria, and Spotted Persicaria. In the pond Water Plantain Alisma. and in the field Bladder Campion and Harebell (Variety) Found a Wasps nest in a hole in the rockery, and the wasps were flitting in and out. Meadow Brown Butterflies in quantities everywhere While we were at lunch, a very large butterfly flitted in for a moment, and as it went out its wings glinted purple in the sunshine. think it must have been a Purple Emperor.

+ July 16th

Early in the morning saw a pair of Turtle Doves strutting up the lane I was just getting the glasses to have a better look at them, when they flew off. They are very slender compared to the Wood Pigeons. - During the night a wind rose, and in the morning a fresh breeze was blowing. This kept the morning comparatively cool. Later clouds came up, but towards evening the sun shone brilliantly, and the atmosphere became very close and heavy as tho' a storm were brewing.

July 18th 1928.

Leaving the house for London at 7.30 AM saw many Whitethroats clinging to the stems of tall Spear Plume Thistles, pecking among the downy heads. Very close day - Towards night windy, with very thundrous atmosphere -

July 19th

Woke to the cooing of London Pigeons. Cloudy and cooler - but very sunny later. From the train saw many baby rabbits scuttling about the fields their vanishing tails flashing white in the sunshine. Saw several pairs of Wood Pigeon. Quantities of Meadow Sweet - and sheets of Rose Bay along the banks of the railway.

July 21st

Very warm again.
Dragon Fly Larva
It moved about when I poked it gently - I hoped it would split its case and emerge, but it was evidently not ready for it crawled under another leaf - In the evening I saw it again, but in the water - The dragon-fly larva changes its skin many times, and lives on flies and insects. Have heard the Woodpeckers often in the Ash tree, but have not actually seen them for some time. "Brave" managed to get into the fruit cage and was very difficult to get out, as when we went in, he came to us and fed quietly at our feet, cheeping cheerfully, and one did not want to frighten him with shoo-ing him out. A night of stars and tiny crescent moon.

Glorious sunny day. Found a sunning itself on a big lily leaf.

July 22nd

A very hot day - Looked for the dragonfly larva, but it has completely dis-appeared - Whilst hunting among the lily leaves a tiny frog leapt into the middle of a very large one, and there he sat enthroned, like the frog prince of the fairy tale

The upper pool is drying out rapidly, and the water lillies are beginning to look unhappy - The bullrushes are festooned with dried green slime - Virginia Creeper is turning colour already. and leaves are falling from the trees. The grass in the orchard is covered with tiny apples, fallen because of the drought. Miss Great Spotted Woodpecker was at the shelter off and on during the day, many young Blackbirds and Thrushes about. In the evening the Spirea was full of Chiff Chaffs or Willow-Warblers. It was difficult to tell which at a distance, not being near enough to see the colour of the legs. In the former these are almost black - and in the latter yellowbrown.

July 23rd

Day very warm again. Was astonished to see the black fish swimming round with one of the Silvers. I wonder if it has been in hiding all these months. or if one of the gold ones has turned black. as last year a gold one changed to silver

July 24th.

Hot and thundery. specks of rain fell twice - I saw a bat flying about just after lunch, it kept darting out from under the eaves, flying round and going in again. At the first glance I thought it was a Swallow. It came out about six times _ Saw one of the Turtle Doves preening itself on the Cottage roof _ they are very tame _

July 25th 1928

Atmosphere very thundery and steamy. clouds _ but no rain. The ground is so dry the birds can get no worms _ they flock to the shelter and to the dining room door, where there is a dish of Osoko which they love. Young Thrushes come repeatedly, and when there is nothing left they stand in the dish! I put out extra bread after lunch on the shelter as there were only a few hard bits left, and the young birds nearly choke themselves in their efforts to gulp them down whole. Blue Tits are beginning to reappear after a long absence.

July 26th

Found an empty Dragonfly larva Case on the lily leaves, and am afraid it was the one I saw in the water the other day. There are six or seven baby frogs in the pond. They climb up the side, and I am sure long to get out. Saw two Peacock Butterflies, and dozens of Small and Large Whites. Meadow Browns and Heaths. An Accentor has been coming for the last two or three days, and this morning he sat on the dish eating Osoko in company with a young Thrush.

July 27th

Woke to the welcome sound of pouring rain about 6 A.M. it was accompanied by distant rolling Thunder. The air was wonderfully fragrant with the scent of the wet earth _ Blackbirds and Thrushes were crowding on the lawn, pecking eagerly for worms _ I saw a Blackbird having a "set to" with two chaffinches over some tasty morsel. On the way to Portsmouth saw Spear Plume Thistle. Common Marjoram, and some lovely big clear pink "Great Bindweed" Fields and Downs were gay with great golden patches of Ragwort, the hedges with trailing Travellers Joy, and the banks with Common Fennel _ Noticed little green chestnuts on the Horse Chestnut trees. It rained off and on all day, and the air grew quite cold.

July 28th

During the night deluges of rain _ but the day was brilliant, clear and delightfully cool. Watched several Willow Warblers on the peasticks and in the orchard, I was able to see their pale brown legs which distinguish them from the Chiffchaff very distinctly. One came on to the bridge, and gathered grasses in his beak _ then he dropped them, then again gathered more, as if he were collecting for a nest, but he finally went off without them. One of them was in the fruit cage, with two chaffinches. His mate outside flew up and down with him in great distress, till at last I got him out, and they flew off joyously together _ Two others had a tremendous fight among the sweetpeas. and rolled on the ground shrieking with rage! They make a curious clicking sound with their wings as they turn in flying and are very swift in their movements. Found Helleborine (Media) in the lane. Fleabane in the garden Yellow Moon and stars.

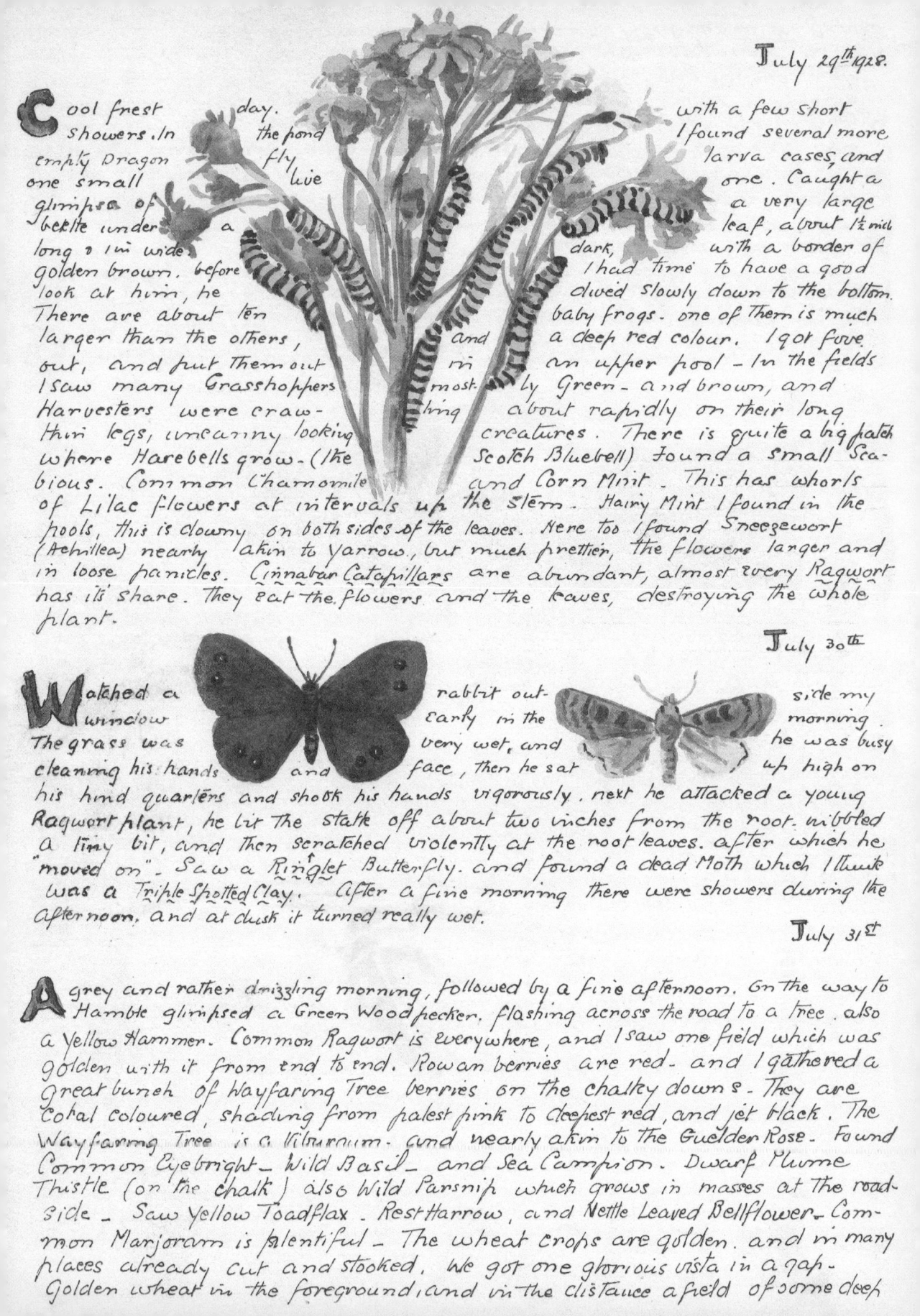

July 29th 1928.

Cool frest day. the pond with a few short
showers. In I found several more
empty Dragon fly live larva cases, and
one small one. Caught a
glimpse of a very large
beetle under a leaf, about 1½ inch
long & 1 in wide dark, with a border of
golden brown. before I had time to have a good
look at him, he dived slowly down to the bottom
There are about ten baby frogs. one of them is much
larger than the others, a deep red colour. I got five
out, and put them out an upper pool - In the fields
I saw many Grasshoppers mostly Green - and brown, and
Harvesters were craw- about rapidly on their long
thin legs, uncanny looking creatures. There is quite a big patch
where Harebells grow - (the Scotch Bluebell) found a small Scabious. Common Chamomile and Corn Mint. This has whorls
of Lilac flowers at intervals up the stem. Hairy Mint I found in the
pools, this is downy on both sides of the leaves. Here too I found Sneezewort
(Achillea) nearly akin to Yarrow., but much prettier, the flowers larger and
in loose panicles. Cinnabar Caterpillars are abundant, almost every Ragwort
has its share. They eat the flowers and the leaves, destroying the whole
plant.

July 30th

Watched a rabbit out- side my
window early in the morning.
The grass was very wet, and he was busy
cleaning his hands and face, then he sat up high on
his hind quarters and shook his hands vigorously. next he attacked a young
Ragwort plant, he bit the stalk off about two inches from the root. nibbled
a tiny bit, and then scratched violently at the root leaves. after which he
"moved on". Saw a Ringlet Butterfly. and found a dead Moth which I think
was a Triple Spotted Clay. After a fine morning there were showers during the
afternoon. and at dusk it turned really wet.

July 31st

A grey and rather drizzling morning, followed by a fine afternoon. On the way to
Hamble glimpsed a Green Woodpecker. flashing across the road to a tree. also
a Yellow Hammer. Common Ragwort is everywhere, and I saw one field which was
golden with it from end to end. Rowan berries are red. and I gathered a
great bunch of Wayfaring Tree berries on the chalky downs. They are
coral coloured, shading from palest pink to deepest red, and jet black. The
Wayfaring Tree is a Viburnum. and nearly akin to the Guelder Rose. Found
Common Eyebright - Wild Basil - and Sea Campion. Dwarf Plume
Thistle (on the chalk) also Wild Parsnip which grows in masses at the roadside - Saw Yellow Toadflax. Rest Harrow, and Nettle Leaved Bellflower- Common Marjoram is plentiful - The wheat crops are golden. and in many
places already cut and stooked. We got one glorious vista in a gap-
Golden wheat in the foreground, and in the distance a field of some deep

mauvey blue flower, topped with vermillion poppies - Found single Harebells and many field Scabious. In the evening whilst gathering Sweet Peas I came across a Small White Butterfly, folded in sleep upon a white Sweet pea - looking for all the world like one of the flowers. Found White Goosefoot in the kitchen garden.

Aug. 1<sup>st</sup> 1928

A thoroughly wet. day - Found Rayless Chamomile and saw a blue butterfly. probably a Common Blue. I find the Beetle I saw in the Lilypond on the 29<sup>th</sup> is a Dytiscus or Carnivorous Beetle. a very voracious creature which devours all small life in the pond, newts, tadpoles etc. and it will even attack a small goldfish. It is winged, and flies from pond to pond at will - arrived at its destination it closes its wing cases, and drops like a stone into the water. It is dark, olive tinged in colour with a light yellow brown border. I went out in the evening to look for mine, and threw in tiny pieces of meat to attract it. but saw no sign of it - I had hoped to see him come up to breathe through his tail !

Aug. 2<sup>nd</sup>

Fine though very overcast at times. Going across country to Henley found Burdock in flower also Lesser Dodder, twined round a stalk like a piece of bright pink thread, with masses of tiny white flowers. Saw a Large Heath Butterfly both male and female, the former being much small- er than the latter Found a young bird on a bark I think it must have been a Meadow Pipit - Brown back under parts whitish, speckled and streaked dark brown. I could have caught it, but did not like to frighten it - and it hopped away into a garden. Saw a Wasp's nest, in some stones. Someone had tried to burn them out, but the wasps were still going in and out. Saw a very beautiful Salmon pink Spear Plume Thistle, quite unlike any others. The whole Country Side is glowing with Rose Bay and Ragwort - Fleabane is abundant, and Hedge Woundwort. We found Eyebright and Ling Heather on The Common and Rest Harrow in a field where a flock of sheep were taking their noonday rest in the shade of a great spreading oak - Found a funny little Caterpillar like a thread half an inch long; which pro- gressed by means of arching its body and bringing its tail to its head Ω, Then moving its head forward ____ to the full extent of its body

Aug 4<sup>th</sup>

Very wet morning, clear- afternoon though not warm. ing at noon, and a lovely or Tree Pipit in the fruit Found a young Meadow bottom, and the mother cage. it was trying to get out at the I went in it forced its way was feeding it through the wire. When inner one I was able to get it between the two wires, and lifting the not like to examine it to make sure out. it was very frightened - so I did which Pipit it was ( the Tree Pipit having the hind claw shorter than the toe and curved for perching on twigs - whereas the Meadow Pipit has the hind claw longer than the toe, and almost straight.) I put it down outside the wire, and in a moment it was gone.

Aug 5th 1928.

A glorious day of sunshine and warmth - I watched a Nuthatch within a few feet of me busily chipping the bark off the rose fence; he was attacking it with great vigour, and pieces were flying all round him - he seemed to be getting a feast of insects from the rotten wood - Willow Warblers were flitting about, one on the top of the shelter two chasing each other in and out of the peasticks, another running over the cage netting. Saw the most beautiful Dragonfly I have ever seen, the head brilliant irridescent green, and the body green, with triangular patches of sapphire blue. Its wings shimmered in the sunlight as it hung suspended from a twig. In the lily pond I found one dead between two leaves. it was a large one, no colour in the body, but patches of white and dark. I wonder if it ever flew, the wings were perfect. Many butterflies about. saw a Peacock - and a Small Tortoiseshell amongst others. Collected a family of snails from the wall, and threw them out for the birds to eat. Already there are red berries for the Yew Tree. Watched a Jay taking a long drink at the Satyrs pool -

Aug. 7th

Found Hop - a non fruit bearing one, with sprays of greenish white flowers. At Easebourne found White Bryony.

Aug. 9th

Pagham.

Found a dead Cinabar Moth ... A glorious day, with a few clouds. Saw Verbascum ... in several places on the way to Pagham. A ... wonderful sunset fleecy clouds tinged with pink ... A lovely starlight night.

Aug 10th

A wonderful morning. At 5.15 AM a host of Gulls settled in the field for a few minutes on their way inland. Followed soon after by Rooks from a tree in the next field. Wood Pigeons were cooing - Heavy dew lay sparkling on the grass, and the sky was pink, which foretold the showery afternoon. On the way to the beach found Horned Poppy There was some Viper's Bugloss near the sea - rather stunted and shrubby also Bedstraw. Swallows fly round as we sit at meals, and afterwards Sparrows flock round to pick up the crumbs.

Aug 11th

A lovely day and the sun very hot. On the way to the beach found a very pretty flower rather like Woody Nightshade. At dusk a heavy mist rolled in from the sea.

Aug 12th

There was a thunderstorm in the night, but we woke to a heavenly day Towards evening a wind got up. Lovely mackerel sky and starlight night.

A very heavy shower about 8AM. and later there was a lovely double rainbow. Still very windy, and the sea rough. Saw a shooting star.

Another lovely day. The Sparrows are very tame, and come into the tents directly we leave them, hunting for cake crumbs.! Watched about six having vigorous baths on a little sand heap by the fire.

### Fernhurst.

Robins are about again in the garden. They have been nesting down in the wood. now they perch about on the well and in the Thorn tree, singing cheerfully. Found a red toad in the lane and helped it on to the bank for fear it should be run over. The hind legs of the toad are much shorter than those of the frog. which are half as long again as the body, enabling him to take high leaps. The toad crawls. and gives little short hops. his body is covered with little bumps.

### Fernhurst - Honiton.

Lovely day, a little overcast and not too hot. Near Petersfield saw a brood of large young pheasants in the road. During the day saw many swallows _____ sitting in rows on the telegraph wires. Wood _____ Pigeons flying across the fields, and in one _____ pasture hosts of Rooks were feeding with a flock of sheep. We came upon a Hedgehog in the road, and passed over it without touching it. The Haw- thorn berries are deep red and The Wayfaring Tree's Scarlet. On The Wiltshire Downs there were masses of little Scrubby bushes, like stunted Cypress Trees. Saw a branch of Elm on which the leaves were turning yellow. the brilliant shades of lemon and orange standing out vividly against the dark green. of the other boughs. In most places the wheat was cut and stooked. but there were several fields of deep golden waving corn, and next to one was a stretch of silvery blue green cabbages. In the hedges the Lesser Bindweed, was climbing, instead of creeping along the Ground, and the pale pink flowers looked like miniature wild roses. Beyond Sherborne the newly ploughed fields were a deep Copper red. I saw bright pink Yarrow.

### Honiton to Paignton.

Patches of rain and sunshine. A very sharp shower about 10.AM. then another about 3.30. A glorious evening with wonderful great billowy cream clouds, suffused apricot. These gradually changed to delicate rose, then as the sun finally disappeared, they faded to cold grey blue on the horizon. By the roadside I saw masses of Tansy with its tight button-like yellow flowers. There was a great deal of Pink Yarrow.

Woke to many a high wind at 5AM, and the cheerful chirp of Sparrows. By 7o/c the wind had dropped. From my window watched two Starlings, two Blackbirds and some Sparrows fighting for crumbs at a back door. Whilst bathing two Swans came sailing up, and were fed by people on the beach. There are a great many Spotted Flycatchers in the hotel garden; they keep darting out from the trees, and circling, twisting and turning, and looping the loop in a most curious way. I saw one with a large fly in its beak. Starlings are plentiful on all the lawns, also Pied Wagtails.

August 22<sup>nd</sup> 1928.

At 6 AM was woken by the screaming of the Gulls, as a large flock of them swooped down on the Esplanade Green — They evidently find many tasty scraps there. They were succeeded by Starlings. It was rather a grey day, and the Flycatchers were tumbling about the lawn, flying very low. I saw a Pied Wagtail strutting about. Two Sparrows had a long thin crust of bread, some starlings came to steal it, but were frightened away by hearing footsteps. There is a huge Cat here in shape he is like a gigantic mole a great fat body on very small legs and paws. and a very tapering tail. It weighs twenty four pounds but is quite active and will jump through clasped hands!

August 23<sup>rd</sup>

A rather grey day with showers and an occasional burst of sunshine. Saw a young Sparrow being fed in the garden. Two Spotted Flycatchers came and sat on the garden wall, within a few feet of the diningroom window. On the newly mown tennis courts I saw many Pied Wagtails feeding. The older birds hovering about the younger, which are greyish in colour. They run along the ground at a tremendous rate, their tails beating up and down incessantly, as if they were on wire springs. This is why in France they are called Washerwomen — after the women who beat their washing on stones at the waters edge.

August 24<sup>th</sup>

Lovely morning followed by a very wet afternoon. About 6 pm it cleared up for a time. The night was wet and wild. Saw a Chiff Chaff in the garden.

August 25<sup>th</sup>

In Torquay I saw many young Common Gulls, perching on row boats in the harbour. They are mottled brown instead of being clear grey white and black like the older birds. The parents hovered round them, and from time to time one would perch on a boat, open its mouth wide, and without moving its bills, utter a series of piercing cries from the throat, without seemingly attracting the slightest notice from the young birds.

August 26<sup>th</sup>

Such a day of rain — it began at 9 AM. and did not let up until about 9.30 PM. Then it cleared slightly, the roads were rivers and there were little ponds on the Esplanade green. Here I saw two birds strange to me. Dunlins, a species of longer than the plumage ash greyish while. tame and seemed to by; even when chased in the air, and fluttered over the ground while bills into the pools of my shoes to go out for a better view of them, but when I came down they had disappeared. – I imagine they were changing from their summer to their winter plumage –

but I think they were Sandpiper. with a little head. dark legs. upper brown. and breast They were marvellously pay no attention to passers dogs they only rose a few inches on a yard or two – They ran feeding, poking their long water. I went up to change

August 27th 1928.

**W**indy but fine till about 6 pm. when it became showery. The sky was very pretty, far above a deep blue with tiny fleecy white clouds. and below them a hurrying transparent veil of clouds, ragged and smokey.

August 28th

**O**ut rowing we watched the young Gulls with their parents. Wherever there was a boat with anyone fishing, there was a little following of Gulls, waiting for any chance scraps to come their way. Saw a gull with only one young one. it seemed very backward it was very fluffy looking, and kept very close to the parent crying incessantly to be fed. In the evening there were short showers – and a rainbow. The sky was lovely at sundown. The fleecy white cirrus clouds being tinged with green and pink as though they were reflecting a rainbow.

August 30th

**A** wonderful day of bright sunshine, and cloud effects. The sea troubled for a time – then still like glass. Fed the Gulls out at sea – They crowded quite near the boat, swooping down on the pieces snatching them as they passed, fighting and screaming at each other. The young ones are very handsome with their dark beaks and mottled plumage –

August 31st

**V**ery fine but the sun overcast, the sea like a mirror. Again fed the Gulls at sea. Saw Common Tern, or sea Swallows as they are called their tails being forked like those of their land namesakes They have little black caps and are much smaller than the Common Gull. Saw Herring Gulls. – great big fellows with an enor- mous expanse of wing In a tiny cove found all kinds of small shell fish. every stone seemed to have several hangers-on. These cling so tenaciously it is impossible to pull them off with the fingers. In the rocks and pools all kinds of odd little creatures ran and swam about. In the hotel garden saw young sparrows being fed. their seem to be a young broods still about. saw a small great many Tortoiseshell Butterfly.

Paignton.                                                  September 1st 1928.

A glorious day. There must be a wasps nest near the hotel, as we are pestered with them in the diningroom. Saw a very curious bird in the hotel garden. it had a thrushes' head and neck, and a completely black blackbirds' body —

September. 3rd.

### Paignton to North Curry.

Another lovely day, with very pretty lights. Scenery rather monotonous. At North Curry there was a brood of baby chicks three days old at the farm where we stayed. Saw a Robin and a Wren sitting on a gate together.

### North Curry to Fernhurst.                    September. 4th

Very warm and lovely day. The trees are beginning to change colour rapidly and I saw many crimson splashes in the hedges. The Hawthorns are thick with berries everywhere, and there are many acorns on the oaks. Nearly all the crops are cut and gathered. I saw only two still standing, and they were oats. Saw Starlings sitting on the sheep's backs, 'pecking, pecking.' The air full of flying thistle down.

September 5th

There are hundreds of wasps about. especially on the lily leaves in the pond. There I saw a very large DragonFly. Emerald green and pale blue. The ivy on the house is covered with flies of all descriptions, which rise in a buzzing swarm as you pass. Tits of all kinds are coming to the shelter, and the Robin is very much in evidence. He sits singing in the trees, and chases the other birds from the shelter — There are still Willow Warblers about.

September 6th

A lovely day, but cooler and overcast at times, a shower of rain in the late evening.          The silver leaves of the White Poplars shimmered and          sparkled against the black lowering clouds in the sky.          Saw a covey of Partridges in the village. Our sun-          flowers are nearly over, and I saw a Marsh          Tit verybusy pecking out the seeds. The nights          are dark. and starlit. and the Owls call to each          other across the valley.

September 9th

Drizzle, and          later tremendously heavy showers, but without thunder. fine at intervals.

September 11th.

On the way to Bognor saw quantities of greater Bindweed. the hedges were full of it. The Willow Herbs are scattering their silvery hairs. and Old Mans Beard is rampant in the hedges. At Midhurst saw Swans and Cygnets. Fields were being ploughed and flocks of gulls were hovering over the newly turned earth. In the garden saw a Red Admiral Butterfly. my first this season.

Saw Martie transfixing a baby Rabbit outside my window. I shouted and clapped my hands. and the noise just lent the Rabbit suffisant courage to tear itself from that petrifying stare and dive into the bushes where it was safe. As I was passing a shop in Haslemere I saw what looked like a tiny leaf blowing towards me. To my amazement discovered it to be a baby House Mouse, the minutest Thing. It ran along aimlessly, sniffing at this and that and in imminent danger of being troddenon by every passer-by. I put my hand down and it ran to me, as if it were tame and when I picked it up, it cuddled down in my hand. as if grateful for the warmth. I finally took it to Miss T. We gave it some cheese and it sat up with a piece in it paws, and nibbled it, then it burrowed down into a glass jar filled with cotton wool, and went to sleep. Found a Solitary Wasp. There are a good many about.

## September 14th

As I was walking down the lane I heard a persistent "tap tap tap" I crept cautiously to the hedge, and peered through into the copse. and there about three feet from me on an oak tree was a Nuthatch hanging head downwards, hammering away at a nut he had wedged into the bark. After about two minutes the shell gave, and picking out the kernel he flew off with it in his beak. Found some lovely fresh Honeysuckle in the lane. Tormentil is still in flower it seems to be an early and late bloomer. Bryony berries are red but the withering leaves rather spoil their effect. Had a Two Spot Ladybird in my window.

## September 15th

Found another Ladybird - this time a Seven Spot. It fell over on it's back on the window sill, and kicked wildly and ineffectually to recover itself. when I touched it, it drew in it's waving legs and pretended to be dead.! When I went out to put bread on the shelter four or five Marsh Tits came fluttering round, to impatient to wait till I had gone. Apples and Pears are being devoured by Wasps, on the ground and on the trees. They excavate great holes, and then crowd into them 9 and 10 at a time, and become drunk with the juice, then they crawl about in a stupor. Saw a Pied Wagtail at the Lily Pond. the first for about two months.

## September 16th

The day began rather grey, but by 10 o/c the sun was shining brilliantly, and it was quite warm. Found a Robin on the back stairs trying to get out by the skylight I opened a window for him, and coaxed him gently to it. He was not in the least alarmed, chirping to me, and cocking his head on one side. He finally paused on the window sill to sing me a farewell song, before he flew out and away to the Plum Tree - A pair of Wood Pigeon were in the garden today, They flew down into the valley when I went out. There were many blackbirds about searching for worms on the lawn. The big Holly Tree has no berries. The one in the hedge has a good many, but very few leaves.

September 17th 1928.

In the village I saw a Swallows nest which had fallen from the roof of a cottage. The nest with four babies had been placed in a basket on a window sill, and here the young were reared by the parents. The basket is covered over with a cloth at night. I saw the parents feeding the little ones, two climbed to the edge of the basket fluttering their wings, then suddenly one seemed to fall in the air, recover its balance, and discover it could fly! It soared upwards, circled and disappeared behind the cottages. The young have soft dark breasts. This brood is a very late one, and one wonders if they will be strong enough to undertake the long journey south at the end of the month. The older birds are already beginning to gather in flocks. Saw a Yellow Brimstone Butterfly in the garden. Robins are everywhere, looking so very "new." with such bright red breasts and such neatly fitting coats. One comes on the porch and to my window, peering in at me and singing a joyous song. I feel it must be the same as the one which sits on a post near the drawingroom door, and sings his little song over and over again. The Robin seems to be the only bird which really sings at the moment - The Blackbirds are very busy on the elderberries, and soon there will be none left.

September 18th

Have never seen so many birds in the garden, as when I looked out of my window before breakfast. Blackbirds and Thrushes hopped about the lawn, and weighed down the slender branches of the Elder Tree, Great Tits and Marsh Tits were running up and down the Rose bushes. Blue Tits flew busily hither and thither, a pair of Cock Chaffinches fought on the wall, watched by a very new-looking Robin - while from the wood came the "tap tap tap" of the Nuthatch. The day began with a dense white mist, which however soon cleared away and gave place to brilliant Sunshine - In the evening found an Angle Shades Moth, in the house.

September 19th.

The day was very grey to begin with, and quite cold, at 9o/c it was drizzling; but it cleared completely and was beautifully fine and warm. A Woodpigeon came to both the Hawthorn and the Elder tree - and ate the berries, I had a splendid view of him - He had great difficulty in balancing himself on the slender branches of the Elder, which bent beneath his weight.

September 20th

Found a Herald Moth in the den, and Golden Rod on a bank in the village. In the early morning I heard two Wrens having a vocal contest, one in the hedge - the other in the wood.

They sang again and again, each waiting to sing till the other had finished. I had not heard them at all for some time, until today. Willow Warblers and Chiff Chaffs have evidently taken their departure as I have seen none for quite a week.

September 22nd.

Met three young Hen Pheasants in the lane. They seemed very tame and not at all anxious to get out of the way, but they never seem to mind a car. Heavy clouds about and the air colder.

September 23rd.

Quite a cold raw day. The sun made many attempts to shine, but without much success. We had our first fire of the season. Near Hind-head saw a Chestnut Tree with golden and vermillion leaves.

September 24th

On Milford Heath saw a Red Squirrel run across the road. I have often seen one at the same spot. A rather raw day with about an hour of drizzling rain in the morning. Owls Calling

September 25th

A cold day. Saw a Green Woodpecker fly across to the dead branches of an Ash Tree at the bottom of the garden. It gave a loud "laugh" as it settled, a curious harsh sound. This laugh gains for the Green Woodpecker the name of "Yaffle" - He is also called "Popinjay" and Wood Sprite.

September 27th.

Saw a fruit also Petty weed- Found

Speckled Wood Butterfly. and found bearing Common Hop in the lane - Spurge - a very common garden Dwarf Furze or gorse.

September 28th

A sudden change in the weather. The night was windy followed by mist and then rain. At midday it was pouring and it did not stop till about 4pm. The birds were very busy worm hunting, and I saw a Wren, the first for a long time, hopping about the bridge and rockery steps. Many birds came to the shelter, Tits, Robins chaffinches etc.

October 2nd.

Found "Robins Pincushions" on Wild Roses. These are formed by Gall Wasps. The "pincushions" are composed of several little hard galls, each one containing a larva. and coated with red and green moss-like hairs -

October 3rd

A pair of House Sparrows made their appearance in the garden, hopping about in the Holly Tree. Sparrows very rarely visit us

I suppose because the house is isolated, and they prefer streets and many rooftops. I have seen them in the garden before, in the winter – but none ever come in the summer. Wasps disappeared almost completely a few days ago. but the sun today was so warm that they swarmed in on us again, many of them in a very sleepy state. and G.M.S. was stung – The night was windy with moonlit strata clouds drifting across the sky, and Owls were calling to each other across the valley.

October 4th 1928.

Found Scentless Mayweed (of the Chamomile family) Also Marsh Cudweed and Marsh Bird's foot Trefoil. House Martins are still flying about in the village.

October 6th

### Fernhurst to Basingstoke.

Leaves changing colour. and falling – a rain of Pine needles in the breeze. Acorns and Chestnuts abundant. Saw Watercress Beds near Basingstoke.

October 7th.

### Basingstoke to Monmouth.

Autumn is more and more advanced the further west we travel Elms are golden, beeches shaded from copper to burnished brass and the thorn bushes glow like red flames in the hedges. I saw masses of shining black Privet berries weighing down the slender branches, and by the roadside Charlock was in full bloom. I saw many flocks of Sparrows in the fields of stubble, and one was black with hundreds of Starlings. Saw a Wood Pigeon seated on a fence post, by the open road, motionless. and as we passed I saw its mate flying across to join it. Near Cirencester I saw a Common Gull hovering over a ploughed field and in the streams I noticed many Moorhens– and a Swan. There were Rooks in large families in the fields The streams in many places were bordered by pollarded willows It rained a good deal and was very close.

October 8th

### Monmouth to Brecon.

Autumn colourings very beautiful. The day was showery with sunny intervals. From the hotel we see the Brecon Beacons 2.900. feet above the sea, The summits were veiled in mist Watched a pair of Jackdaws beating their way to windward, and like aeroplanes taking advantage of the varying currents in the air. There are many Jackdaws round the hotel.

### Brecon.
October 9th

Such a curious day of April showers. The effect of sunshine and shadows drifting across the Beacons was beautiful.

Woke to the cawing of Jackdaws, then heard a Robin and a Wren singing - Saw Robins, Chaffinches and House Sparrows in the garden. The old Ely Tower is covered with deep green Ivy in flower. against which the Virginia creeper glows a brilliant crimson. There are three kinds of "Virginia" the tiny leaved Ampelopsis - the large leaved. and the third a delicate trailing kind, the leaves instead of being palmate are divided right back to the stalk. On the roof of the Tower I found Ivy leaved Toadflax ← Maidenhair Spleenwort and Wall Rue

Spleenwort
chimney to
wide stack
was
of it
right down into
there were a
go down, then

Watched the Jackdaws flying from
chimney One pair settled on a
from which
pouring,
the birds
the chimney,
nest there. One
when it emerged the

smoke
in spite
went
as if
would
other

would disappear into the smoke. There is a funny little tabby cat here with very large ears and great round eyes in a very small head. The thumb and first finger of her front paws are joined together in a large blob - the maid says she was born so and all her kittens are the same.

### Brecon to Hereford                    October 10th 1928.

At 6.30 AM there was a tremendous cawing, and looking out I saw a great flock of Jackdaws wheeling and circling round the old tower They seemed to be holding some kind of meeting, before all going off for the day to their various chimney pots and tree tops., A little later two birds locked in combat hurled themselves at my window - I think they were Robins for I heard some scolding below, just round the corner out of sight. Watched a Wren creeping like a mouse in and out of the Ivy on the old wall. As we went over the mountains to Rhayader we saw a flock of quite one hundred or more Plovers - high overhead. (Green Plover. Lapwing, or Peewit) I wonder if they had just arrived from the North, to winter here. The dying Bracken on the Hills is a wonderful colour, gold and bronze in the sunshine. Saw "Snow Berries" The Rowan Trees are a glorious crimson with vermillion berries, and the Dogwoods are a glowing scarlet among the other Trees. I saw a hen with chicks about two weeks old, a very late brood. The Welsh ponies are sweet - small and stocky with flowing mane and tail. This seems to be a Jackdaw Country for they are everywhere. I also saw many Rooks, and Common Crows. Near Hereford Meadow Sweet was still in bloom, and I saw a field of Mustard in full flower.

### Hereford to Banbury.        October 11th.

The soil in Wales and Hereford is dark red, very much as it is in Devonshire, it seems to be very heavy to work, as I saw four and five horses in single file to a single furrow plough, and three horses abreast to a harrow. Many Pear and Apple trees are still covered with fruit, especially the little bright red apples. As we were coming into Stowe on the Wold, on a quiet piece of road a Fox sud - denly darted out. Got half way across, saw us, and ran back, leaping lightly over a stone wall into a turnip field. He was such a beauty, with a glossy red coat and great bushy tail, with a white tip.

October 12th 1928.

Banbury to Farnham.

There was a wonderful Wistaria on the White Lion Hotel at Banbury. About 300 years old it stretches its branches to about 50 yards on either side of the main stem which is well over a yard in circumference. At Reading I found Knot grass. — Here at the Bush Hotel Farnham there are dozens of sparrows in the garden, pecking about among the fallen leaves, while Blackbirds are busy eating the Hawthorn berries — A Common Crow came sneak- ing in, but was frightened away by the sparrows! There are some very curious pigeons here — with red-bronze head neck and underbody. while the wings and entire back are irredescent green - black.

October 13th

Farnham to Fernhurst-

At Frensham Ponds at 9.AM the Swans were all drawn up on a little sandy stretch, by the water, making their morning toilette, stretching their long necks and preening their feathers, in the faint morning sunshine - It was bleak and cold on the common. And the first chill of real winter was in the air. We found an Earwig in the Village Hall!

October 15th

Much warmer again, and many wasps revived and came in to the house flying low - and almost noiselessly.

October 21st

The last few days we have had rain at some time each day. Today has been one of wind, rain, sunshine and hail - in the after- noon there was a wonderful double rainbow - the inner bow remained clear and intact for more than half an hour.

October 22nd

Another day of torrents of rain with intervals of brilliant sunshine. Again there was a double rainbow. Saw the Greater Spotted Woodpecker on the shelter, the first time for weeks.

October 23rd 1928

A lovely day till evening, when a gale rose, and there was some rain. Saw two cock Pheasants with a hen between them, sitting on the top rail of the gate into the wood.

October 25th

While I was dressing Nicco came crying pitifully down the passage, I let him in, and sitting down by the fireplace, he looked up into my face crying continuously. I found he had a rabbit snare wound tightly round the ankle of the right front paw. I ran for H.T.S, and he soon got the wire off with pliers – poor Nicco cried with pain, and wriggled but never attempted to bite or scratch, and was so grateful. I carried him to G.M.S's fire, and laid him in front of it – he lay still completely exhausted – The paw was terribly stiff and swollen, also the whole leg, but he was soon able to stand my gently rubbing it, and loudly purred his gratitude. He had some milk, then lay all day sleeping with meals at intervals. He slept the night on my bed.

October 26th

Much rain at intervals and raging wind.

October 28th.

Nicco's paw is perfectly normal again, but the accident has I think rather shaken his nerve! and he likes to be with us and lie all day by the fire. He was very annoyed to find none lit in the drawingroom this morning, and came crying to me in the garden room, where I was planting bulbs in bowls. Then he went and cried to G.M.S in the hall. and unable to resist his pleading she lit the fire for him! He refused to go out last thing, and crept into my lap purring, so I allowed him to sleep on my bed again.

October 29th

A wonderful sunrise, followed by greyness, then alternate sunshine and rain. Found a young rat dead by the birds shelter, evidently laid there by Nicco.

October 30th

After a sharp shower the weather cleared and the sun shone brilliantly Bryony Berries are thick in the hedges in the lane. Ragwort Hogweed, White Dead Nettle and Knapweed are still in flower – also Common Sow Thistle and Hawkweed. Jays were making a great noise in the field.

October 31st

It was showery, and there was a rainbow. Found Herb Robert and Campion still in bloom in the lane – Saw two plovers flying over the valley.

November 6th 1928

On our way to Guildford saw two Swans on the wing – but they were to far away for us to hear the music of their wings. At night it turned very cold indeed.

November 10th.

Woke to find the ground white with frost. It was very cold in the morning but grew quite warm towards evening – Found yet another goldfish has turned silver!

November 12th

A hopelessly wet and windy day: at times a thick mist enveloped Blackdown and the valley. The wind roared in the chimneys – and the air was warm and heavy.

November 13th

Sunshine and rain – in the passage –            Found a male Winter Moth.

November 14th.

Lovely day until about            6pm when it began to rain. The country on the way to Steyning was glorious in the sunshine. Many Oaks are still quite green – Saw a fat Toad laboriously crossing the road.

November 16th

A terrible day of rain and storm. It poured with rain from early dawn – then towards 11 o/c it cleared for about an hour, the sun shone, in a blue sky. The wind dropped – then the wind blew harder than ever at times the whole house shook with the force of the gale – Rain descended in torrents and penetrated onto the window sills. Then quite suddenly all was still, and stars shone dimly in a clouded sky. Great damage was done all over the country – and many lives were lost at sea –

November 17th

It was raining before 7o/c, then the sky cleared – and the day was lovely Found a Queen Wasp in the drawingroom, but it flew out just before I could kill it. The Gale of yesterday has swept all the tallest trees bare of their leaves, but some of the sheltered Oaks in the valley are still fully clad in their russet brown.

November 18th

A lovely day, though a little cloudy towards evening. In spite of the storm there are still many leaves left on the trees – Ashes are bare, but Oaks in places are still quite green. The bare upper branches of the Elms with their few remaining golden leaves were silhouetted against a deep blue sky, and the sun turned the russet leaves of the Oaks to gold, against the deep green ivy clad trunks. Near Milford Common the silver Birches were leafless, and their slender upright red branches were like a delicate rosy mist among the fir Trees. I saw no Holly berries any where.

November 19th 1928.

The morning was fine, but at midday the wind rose, and in the afternoon rain fell at intervals. In Ropes Lane at 6.30 pm. Tawny and I saw a large bird fluttering above the road in front of us. Tawny exclaimed "A White Owl!" and we ran forward to see it dive into the hedge. Tawny's Cat also saw it, but we arrived in time to sieze him. The bird was a fine Cock Pheasant, he was dazed with the light of our torches, and crouched motionless while we stroked his back. Then we left him in peace - Tawny taking her cat in -

November 20th

A fine day with local showers. On the way to Brighton saw many trees down after the storms. At 2.45 there was a deluge of rain lasting about ten minutes, but the sun never ceased to shine. It was windy by the sea, and big rollers were breaking on the beach. Saw Fieldfares in the marshy meadows round Pullborough. The Fieldfare is an inch less in length than the Missel Thrush - and is distinguishable from the latter by its ash grey head and back. It is also gregarious, and feeds only in wide, open spaces, where it is safe from attacks of any kind. As we were nearing Fernhurst in the dusk, a small bird struck the car, and must have been killed instantly. It is curious how blind birds are directly the light fades.

November 21st

Hopelessly wet and windy. Tits flocked to the shelter all the morning, Great - Blue - and Marsh. while Chaffinches and Blackbirds hopped about underneath, picking up the bread the Tits threw down. At one moment there were six great Tits on the shelter at once. About 11.30 a Cock Bull Finch appeared in the Spirea. He remained for about an hour, then disappeared, returning shortly with Mrs B, who sat in a dejected heap, finding the seeds too wet for her liking - The Great Spotted Woodpecker was clinging to the rustic gate below - hammering vigorously at the bark - and sending chips flying all round him. Saw a Missel Thrush in the orchard. Rain continued all day, almost without ceasing.

November 22nd

Another wet windy day. No Bullfinches in the Spirea - The two who came yesterday, have probably gone off to tell the others the seeds are ripe.

November 23rd.

The wettest and windiest day of all. It poured without ceasing from early dawn till tea time, when the sky cleared. Above one could see golden fleecy clouds, in a blue sky. While below them great smokey clouds scurried before the gale. The night was moonlit.

November 24th 1928.

A complete hush after the storm. The sun shone brilliantly, and it was quite warm. At 4.30 a brilliant moon was shining – The night was very still, and owls were calling across the valley.

November 25th.

The morning was wet – but in the afternoon the sun came out. A strong wind blew all day Mr and Mrs Bullfinch came to the Spirea again. The night was lovely, and when I looked out last thing I surprised two rabbits feeding in the moonlight at the foot of the wall.

November 26th

A glorious day and much colder. Found two common Daisies in the garden. and Pink Campion. Brilliant moon, veiled later by fleecy silver clouds.

November 29th.

Saw the Great Spotted Woodpecker on the shelter.

December 1st.

A Blue Tit inspected the nest on the pergola. He sat for quite a long time – looking in.

December 2nd.

Dawn brought distressed cries from many pheasants in the valley, as they flew up and down, perhaps searching for their mates, victims of yesterdays slaughter. Owls too, were making a great noise. On the road to Godalming I saw a Pied Wagtail, strutting round a small woolley dog in the roadway; They were evidently friends for the bird was within three feet of the dog – At dusk I watched a Cock Pheasant going to roost in our copse – He gave a loud cry each time he hopped from one branch to another – At breakfast time I saw a Nuthatch creep along the wall and hide a piece of bread in a crevisse – he tried two, before he found a suitable one – he pushed it in, then gave it an extra poke to push it out of sight. A moment later I saw him flying in the opposite direction with another piece. Curiously enough, at lunchtime I saw him return to the wall to collect the piece he had hidden there.

December 4th

In the morning I saw Mr Great Spotted Woodpecker hanging on the fat on the shelter, together with a Great Tit. He was about a good deal in the orchard. Three pair of Bullfinch came to the Spirea in the late afternoon – they eat very deliberately, bending slowly down – taking a peck. and returning equally slowly to an upright position. They are very shy. and fly off into the laurels at the first hint of anyones approach,

December 6th

Cold grey day. with drizzling rain. On the way home from Guildford, noticed many small moths fluttering in the light from the car lamps. probably Winter Moths

A second lovely day, with a thick white frost. Saw a large flock of about thirty Wood Pigeons down in the Copse.

December 9<sup>th</sup>

Woke to find the world white with frost. it was very cold. and in the shade great patches of frost remained all day, Though in the sunshine it was quite warm. Three pair of Bullfinch came to the Spirea. All the birds were very hungry, and flocked to be fed. Again I saw the Woodpigeons down in the copse at the same hour as yesterday.

December 10<sup>th</sup>

Very hard frost. The day fine but stormy looking. and bitterly cold. The three pair of Bullfinch were again in the Spirea.

December 11<sup>th</sup>

It rained almost without ceasing all day, and was very cold indeed. The 3 pair Bullfinch again in the Spirea. All birds very hungry and a Jay came for bread.

December 12<sup>th</sup>

It began to snow in the night, and continued till about 11AM. when it turned to sleet and then rain. It was cold and damp. Three pairs of Bullfinches were in the Spirea all day.

December 15<sup>th</sup>

Threw out of my window the inside of a dried up Cocoanut. it rolled under the shrubs where it was at once discovered by a Robin, after which many Tits came. and even Blackbirds, and a Jay, hovered round it. Watched a Wren creeping along the wall. in and out of the crannies like a tiny mouse. Saw a Starling in the orchard.

December 16<sup>th</sup>

Dull and windy turning to rain in the afternoon. I decorated a Christmas tree for the birds, with fat, bones, cocoanut rings and peanuts topped with a half Cocoanut shell filled with hemp seeds and millet. Tits began to come at once, and one could literally see the spreading of the good news. all kinds of birds flocked to the tree. A Marsh Tit came time after time, taking three and more seeds at a time, our Blue Tit was very belligerent, and kept all others at bay while he was there. The Nuthatch came several times. and a Robin managed to perch on a branch to nibble the fat. There was one pair of Bullfinches in the Spirea of which nearly all the seeds have now been eaten. They came down on to the wall. so I put out a trail of hemp seeds, from them to the tree, but a host of noisy Chaffinches discovered the trail and the bullfinches remained in the background, They are very shy birds. A Hedge Sparrow was pecking about, and down the steps. About 11 AM I saw a flock of hundreds of Wood pigeons down in the valley. several large trees were grey with them.

December 17<sup>th</sup>

Quite a lovely day and much warmer, no wind and the sun shining. At night a bright new Crescent Moon & Stars. I see Orion very plainly from my window [E] with Syrius at his heels. and The Bull above him. Saw only one Bullfinch today but think Mr B must have been about somewhere about. as they always go in pairs. There was a constant run on the hemp seeds on the Christmas Tree. I saw the Nuthatch there many times. On the way home from Guildford saw a mouse scuttling across the road. and there were many moths about.

December 18th 1928

**A**ll day long there was a dense mist, with a watery sun gleaming at intervals, trying to penetrate the blanket of fog. In the afternoon the sun looked like a pale silver moon. It was very cold. Saw only Mrs Bullfinch in the Spirea.

December 19th

**S**uddenly heard an unaccustomed bird note, and looking out saw a Long Tailed Tit in the Oak opposite my window. He was alone and soon darted off again. Saw thirty two Wood Pigeons flying up the valley, and many others were perched in the trees.

December 21st.

**A** lovely day, and colder after the mildness of yesterday. The Marsh Tits are very bold. I was gardening just underneath the tree yet they continued to come in quick succession, a little hurried at first, but soon quite at their ease. The water in the lily pond is very clear, and the 14 fish are easily seen. A few wallflower are in bloom. also scraps of Veronica and Campanula. Found a Bulbous Buttercup. and groundsel. The Bullfinches have ceased coming to the Spirea.

December 22nd

**M**iserably misty wet day. Saw birds going to roost early. Now that the trees are bare many nests show up in hedge and copse.

December 23rd.

**L**ovely day and I was able to garden, morning and afternoon. though the ground was very wet. Saw two Long Tailed Tits in the Oak Tree. They were making a great to do. Martie had a mouse in the garden.

December 28th

**H**eavenly morning. About 8AM I heard a great disturbance down in the copse. a beating of wings and muffled cries. Thought it must be a pheasant in a trap. went down to investigate, and put up several pheasants which were feeding near the top. Heard no more flutterings, and suddenly saw Nieeo, striding up from the valley tail in air, delighted to see me. I wondered if he had had a pheasant, or if the sounds came from two Cock Pheasants fighting. Found clumps of Primroses in full flower, though very

short stalked. and thick green carpets of Ground ivy leaves.
The Nuthatch comes a great deal to the Hemp seeds, and takes
his time collecting a mouthful, no other birds dare to come
while he is there. At 4pm it began to rain, and the wind
rose to a gale. Stormy night.

### December 28th

A dreary day of mist and rain. Crowds of birds on the tree
The Chaffinches have learnt to perch on the "hemp cocoanut." and were very busy with the rape seeds which none
of the other birds will touch. I hung an apple on the tree —
the Great Tit eyed it longingly, but did not venture to attack it.

### December 29th

Such a glorious day. On our way to town I saw a Kestrel
hovering — At Godalming all the low fields were flooded
and a pair of Swans were enjoying the water. I noticed
beyond Farncombe that the Hawthorns were crimson with
berries — there always seem to be a great many there, yet I
have never seen a single bird eating them. At Wisley two
Canadian Geese were preening themselves at the edge of
the pond. Everything was bathed in sunshine, dew sparkled on the grass, and the delicate birch boles gleamed
silver among the deep green firs. Round Kingston, Gulls
were flocking in the fields.

### December 30th

In Soho Square I saw a flock of Starlings wheeling and
settling in a tall tree with a great deal of loud Chatter
which they kept up incessantly.

### December 31st

Cold and drizzly in the early morning. It cleared later
and the night was glorious. As the Old Year died a
silvery moon veiled by delicate fleecy clouds rose in the heavens
to greet the New Year    1929.

# Index of Flora and Fauna

Names of species appear as the author wrote them in her journals; the name in parentheses following some of them
is the modern common name, where this differs, or where the author's identification was incorrect. Index entries in
*italic* print refer to an illustration; names in *italics* are scientific names. Dates are given in UK format
(day/month/year), thus 4.7.28 represents 4th July 1928.

## BIRDS

Accentor (Dunnock) 26.7.28.

Blackbird 27.10.26, 21.11.26, *23.11.26*, 1.12.26, 16.12.26, 22.3.27,
26.3.27, 8.4.27, 10.4.27, 26.4.27, 27.4.27, 28.4.27, 29.4.27,
30.4.27, 2.5.27, 8.5.27, 30.5.27, 1.6.27, 26.6.27, 18.9.27,
5.11.27, 27.11.27, 4.12.27, 12.12.27, 19.12.27, 22.1.28, 25.2.28,
1.3.28, 24.3.28, 19.4.28, 21.4.28, 22.4.28, *23.4.28*, 20.5.28,
21.5.28, 1.7.28, 3.7.28, 22.7.28, 27.7.28, 21.8.28 (in journal as
24.8.28), 1.9.28, 16.9.28, 17.9.28, 18.9.28, 12.10.28, 21.11.28,
15.12.28.

Black Cap (Blackcap) *26.4.28*.

Bullfinch *28.11.26*, 16.12.26, 11.11.27, 19.11.27, 22.11.27,
27.11.27, 18.12.27, 23.12.27, *8.2.28*, *18.2.28*, 21.11.28,
22.11.28, 25.11.28, 4.12.28, 9.12.28, 10.12.28, 11.12.28,
12.12.28, 16.12.28, 17.12.28, 18.12.28, 21.12.28.

Canary (silver breed) *13.1.28*.

Chaffinch 25.10.26, 23.11.26, *16.12.26*, 26.4.27, 28.4.27, 1.5.27,
2.5.27, 15.5.27, 13.6.27, 19.6.27, 23.6.27, 24.6.27, 26.6.27,
29.6.27, 3.7.27, 4.7.27, 4.8.27, 18.9.27, 5.11.27, 30.12.27,
19.1.28, 22.1.28, 20.2.28, 23.2.28, 1.3.28, 16.4.28, 21.4.28,
23.4.28, 26.4.28, 19.5.28, 3.6.28, 23.6.28, 24.6.28, 25.6.28,
9.7.28, 10.7.28, 12.7.28, 21.7.28, 27.7.28, 28.7.28, 18.9.28,
28.9.28, 9.10.28, 21.11.28, 16.12.28, 28.12.28.

Chiff Chaff (Chiffchaff) 24.6.28, 22.7.28, 28.7.28, 24.8.28,
20.9.28.

Cormorant *14.7.27*, 18.7.27, 11.8.27, 21.3.28, 22.3.28.

Crow/Common Crow (Carrion Crow) 20.1.28, 10.3.28, 26.3.28,
3.6.28, 8.6.28, 10.10.28, *12.10.28*; Hooded *19.7.27*.

Cuckoo 5.5.27, 12.4.28, *16.4.28*, 25.4.28, 11.6.28, 12.6.28,
25.6.28, 30.6.28, 1.7.28, 6.7.28 (in journal as 6.6.28).

Curlew *18.7.27*.

Dove, Ring (Wood Pigeon) 9.1.28, 17.1.28, 24.3.28;
Stock 26.5.28; Turtle *16.7.28*, 24.7.28.

Duck, Wild (Mallard) 8.5.27, 3.10.27, 10.3.28.

Dunlin *26.8.28*.

Fieldfare *20.11.28*.

Flycatcher, Spotted/Flycatcher (Spotted Flycatcher) 5.5.27,
*12.6.27*, 24.7.27, 10.5.28, 13.5.28, 21.5.28, 10.7.28, 21.8.28
(in journal as 24.8.28), 22.8.28, 23.8.28.

Gannet 18.7.27, *19.7.27*.

Geese, Canadian (Canada Goose) 29.12.28.

Goldfinch *28.11.26*, 6.7.28 (in journal as 6.6.28).

Grouse, Red *16.7.27*, 22.7.27.

Guillemot *18.7.27*, 19.7.27.

Gull, Brown-headed (Black-headed Gull) *13.7.27*, 15.7.27,
16.7.27, 27.7.27; Common White (Common Gull) *13.7.27*,
*4.1.28*, 25.8.28, 31.8.28, 7.10.28; Herring *31.8.28*; Lesser
Black-backed *19.7.27*.

Hawk, Sparrow (Sparrowhawk) *17.7.27*, 21.2.28, 26.5.28,
19.6.28.

Hen, domestic 6.3.28, 3.9.28, 10.10.28.

Heron (Grey Heron) *20.7.27*, *22.7.27*.

Jackdaw 14.7.27, *15.7.27*, 22.7.27, 27.7.27, 26.1.28, 3.6.28,
22.6.28, 8.10.28, 9.10.28, 10.10.28.

Jay *11.6.27*, 26.6.27, 2.9.27, 21.2.28, 8.6.28, 14.6.28, 16.6.28,
17.6.28, 18.6.28, 23.6.28, 1.7.28, 5.7.28 (in journal as 5.6.28),
10.7.28, 11.7.28, 6.8.28, 30.10.28, 11.12.28, 15.12.28.

Kestrel 21.2.28, *26.5.28*, 5.7.28 (in journal as 5.6.28), 29.12.28.

Lark, Sky (Skylark) *14.7.27*, 20.6.28.

Magpie 20.2.28, 22.2.28, 26.3.28, 1.4.28, 4.6.28, 5.6.28, 6.6.28,
8.6.28, 11.6.28, 16.6.28, 17.6.28, 18.6.28, 20.6.28.

Martin, House *28.6.27*, 23.5.28, 25.5.28, 7.6.28, 9.6.28, 17.6.28,
21.6.28, 22.6.28, 4.10.28; Sand 23.5.27.

Moorhen *16.3.27*, 30.6.27, 15.12.27, 18.1.28, 5.3.28, 10.3.28,
7.10.28.

Nightingale 11.5.28.

Nuthatch 16.12.26, 6.4.27, 8.4.27, 31.5.27, 1.6.27, 2.6.27, 26.6.27,
4.8.27, 18.9.27, 22.1.28, 8.2.28, 14.2.28, 27.2.28, 2.3.28,
17.3.28, 24.3.28, 25.3.28, 4.4.28, 8.4.28, 10.4.28, 14.4.28,
16.4.28, 14.5.28, 18.5.28, 20.5.28, 25.5.28, 28.5.28, 1.6.28,
2.6.28, 17.6.28, 6.8.28, *14.9.28*, 18.9.28, 2.12.28, 16.12.28,
17.12.28, 28.12.28.

Owl, Brown (Tawny Owl) 15.2.27, 7.12.27, *12.1.28*, 6.9.28.

Owls 18.11.26, 15.9.27, 5.11.27, 17.1.28, 19.2.28, *12.6.28*,
16.6.28, 24.9.28, 3.10.28, 24.11.28, 2.12.28.

Partridge (Grey Partridge) *6.9.28*.

Peewit/Green Plover (Lapwing) 16.7.27, 17.7.27, 8.4.28.

Petrel, Fulmar (Fulmar) *19.7.27*.

Pheasant *4.12.26*, 13.10.27, 27.11.27, 13.2.28, *14.2.28*, 26.2.28,
22.3.28, 1.4.28, 27.4.28, 29.5.28, 19.8.28, 22.9.28, 23.10.28,
19.11.28, 2.12.28, 28.12.28.

Pigeon (Domestic/Feral Pigeon) *21.3.27*, *15.5.27*, 27.7.27,
23.5.28, 12.10.28; London (Feral Pigeon) 19.7.28; Wood
*17.9.27*, 14.10.27, 26.1.28, 21.2.28, 26.2.28, 14.7.28, 15.7.28,
16.7.28, 19.7.28, 10.8.28, 19.8.28, 16.9.28, 19.9.28, 7.10.28,
8.12.28, 9.12.28, 16.12.28, 19.12.28.

Pipit, Meadow 2.8.28; Meadow/Tree *4.8.28*.

Plover (Lapwing) 19.7.27, 22.7.27, 23.7.27, 10.7.28, 14.7.28,
10.10.28, 31.10.28.

Puffin 19.7.27.

Razor Bill (Razorbill) 19.7.27.

Robin *18.11.26*, 21.11.26, 1.5.27, 26.6.27, 4.8.27, 18.9.27,
24.10.27, *13.11.27*, 17.11.27, *18.11.27*, 20.11.27, 28.11.27,
*17.12.27*, 23.12.27, 29.12.27, 30.12.27, 8.1.28, 22.1.28, 23.2.28,
*23.4.28*, 7.5.28, *14.5.28*, 20.5.28, 26.5.28, 27.5.28, 18.8.28,
3.9.28, 5.9.28, 16.9.28, 17.9.28, 18.9.28, 28.9.28, 9.10.28,
10.10.28, 15.12.28, 16.12.28.

Rook 14.7.27, *23.1.28*, 20.2.28, 10.3.28, 24.3.28, 26.3.28, 26.4.28,
10.8.28, 19.8.28, 7.10.28, 10.10.28.

Snipe *18.7.27*, 20.7.27.

Sparrow (House Sparrow) 10.10.27, 12.10.27, 26.10.27, 25.1.28,
26.3.28, 10.8.28, 7.10.28, 9.10.28; Hedge/Accentor
(Dunnock) *18.12.27*, 28.12.27, 18.3.28, *23.4.28*, 16.12.28;
House *11.7.27*, 13.1.28, 22.1.28, 7.2.28, 4.3.28, 5.3.28, 24.3.28,
25.3.28, 15.8.28, 21.8.28 (in journal as 24.8.28), 22.8.28,
23.8.28, 31.8.28, 3.10.28, 7.10.28, 12.10.28; Tree *10.10.27*,
5.11.27, 13.1.28.

Starling *17.3.27*, *7.7.27*, 25.7.27, 12.11.27, 27.12.27, 28.12.27,
30.12.27, 20.1.28, 22.1.28, 8.3.28, 21.3.28, 4.9.28, 7.10.28,
15.12.28, 30.12.28.

Swallow 28.6.27, 2.7.27, *12.7.27*, 22.7.27, 19.9.27, 3.6.28, 4.6.28,
17.6.28, 20.6.28, 26.6.28, 24.7.28, 10.8.28, *19.8.28*, 21.8.28
(in journal as 24.8.28), 22.8.28, 17.9.28.

Swan, Mute 3.10.27, 18.1.28, 10.3.28, 25.4.28, 16.5.28, 21.8.28
(in journal as 24.8.28), 11.9.28, 7.10.28, 13.10.28, 6.11.28,
29.12.28; Whooper 19.8.27, 15.12.27.

Swans *19.8.27*, 22.2.28.

Swift 3.6.28, 4.6.28, 17.6.28, 11.7.28.

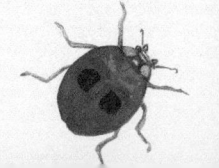

Tern, Common *13.7.27*, 31.8.28.
Thrush, Missel (Mistle Thrush) 25.10.26, 21.3.27, 10.4.27,
    4.6.27, 7.9.27, *18.9.27*, 1.12.27, 1.7.28, 21.11.28; Song
    *21.3.27*, 18.9.27, 22.1.28, 23.1.28, *18.2.28*, 20.2.28, 21.2.28,
    22.2.28, 25.2.28, 1.3.28, 24.3.28, 22.4.28, *23.4.28*, 26.4.28,
    7.5.28, 9.5.28, 11.5.28, 20.5.28, 3.6.28, 3.6.28, 22.7.28, 25.7.28.
Tit, Blue 23.11.26, *26.6.27*, 4.7.27, 3.8.27, 4.8.27, 19.12.27,
    22.1.28, 8.2.28, 20.2.28, *27.2.28*, 6.3.28, 21.3.28, 14.4.28,
    16.4.28, 26.5.28, 25.7.28, 18.9.28, 21.11.28, 16.12.28; Cole
    (Coal Tit) 1.8.27, 13.10.27, *11.11.27*, 22.1.28, 1.12.28; Great
    26.6.27, *29.6.27*, 4.8.27, 12.11.27, 23.12.27, *16.1.28*, 17.1.28,
    22.1.28, 30.1.28, *7.2.28*, 6.3.28, 21.3.28, 21.4.28, 12.5.28,
    14.5.28, 21.5.28, 25.5.28, 28.5.28, 31.5.28, 2.7.28, 3.7.28,
    4.7.28, 6.7.28 (in journal as 6.6.28), 7.7.28 (in journal as
    7.6.28), 18.9.28, 21.11.28, 28.12.28; Long-tailed *31.10.27*,
    22.1.28, 27.3.28, 4.12.28, 19.12.28; Marsh *1.8.27*, 11.11.27,
    15.1.28, 16.1.28, 17.1.28, *1.2.28*, 8.2.28, 21.3.28, 6.9.28,
    15.9.28, 18.9.28, 16.12.28, 21.12.28.
Tree Creeper (Treecreeper) *22.1.28*, 26.1.28, 18.3.28.
Wagtail, Grey *13.10.27*, 2.4.28, 17.6.28; Pied 22.3.27, 11.7.27,
    23.12.27, 27.12.27, 28.12.27, 21.3.28, 21.8.28 (in journal as
    24.8.28), 22.8.28, 23.8.28, 15.9.28.
Warbler, Willow *9.7.28*, 22.7.28, 28.7.28, 6.8.28, 5.9.28, 20.9.28,
    2.12.28.
Whitethroat *3.6.27*, 24.7.27, 9.7.28, 9.7.28, 17.7.28.
Woodpecker, Great Spotted / Greater Spotted (Great Spotted
    Woodpecker) *7.6.28*, 12.6.28, 13.6.28, 1.7.28, 3.7.28, 5.7.28
    (in journal as 5.6.28), 6.7.28 (in journal as 6.6.28), 7.7.28
    (in journal as 7.6.28), 8.7.28, 9.7.28, 10.7.28, 11.7.28, 15.7.28,
    21.7.28, 22.7.28, 22.10.28, 21.11.28, 26.11.28, 4.12.28;
    Green 25.8.27, 17.6.28, 18.6.28, 20.6.28, 31.7.28, 25.9.28.
Wren *20.12.26*, 3.6.27, 11.6.27, 19.6.27, 24.10.27, 6.12.27,
    *17.12.27*, 27.12.27, 14.2.28, 1.3.28, 5.3.28, 6.3.28, 16.3.28,
    18.3.28, 24.3.28, 27.3.28, 1.4.28, 9.4.28, 26.4.28, 27.4.28,
    23.6.28, 3.9.28, 20.9.28, 28.9.28, 9.10.28, 10.10.28, 15.12.28;
    Golden-crested (Goldcrest) 2.5.27.
Yellow Hammer / 'Yellow Bunting' (Yellowhammer) *2.7.27*,
    25.7.27, 29.7.27, 4.6.28, 19.6.28, 20.6.28, 31.7.28.

## MAMMALS

Bats 10.4.28, 24.7.28.
Cat 11.3.27, 24.3.27, 25.3.27, 30.4.27, 11.6.27, 25.6.27, 17.7.27,
    26.9.27, 23.12.27, 28.12.27, *14.2.28*, 18.3.28, 1.4.28, 27.5.28,
    31.5.28, 22.8.28, 9.10.28, 25.10.28, 28.10.28, 29.10.28,
    19.11.28, 28.12.28.
Deer 22.10.26.
Dog 20.3.27, 16.12.27, 2.12.28.
Fox 11.10.28.
Hare (Brown Hare) *19.7.27*.
Hedgehog *19.8.28*.
Horses / ponies 31.12.27, 11.10.28.
Mole 24.11.26, 13.2.28; molehill *13.2.28*.
Mouse, Field (Wood Mouse) 15.7.28; House 13.9.28.
Pig 27.5.28.
Pony, Welsh 10.10.28.
Rabbit 24.2.27, *11.3.27*, *12.3.27*, 31.5.27, 4.6.27, 25.6.27, 16.7.27,
    17.7.27, 31.10.27, 7.12.27, *14.2.28*, 10.3.28, 11.3.28, 18.3.28,
    22.3.28, 1.4.28, 8.4.28, 15.5.28, 18.5.28, 20.5.28, 27.5.28,
    23.6.28, 26.6.28, 6.7.28 (in journal as 6.6.28), 10.7.28, 19.7.28,
    30.7.28, 13.9.28, 25.11.28.
Rat (Brown Rat) 24.2.27, 25.3.27, 9.4.28, 29.10.28.
Sheep / Lambs 17.3.27, *20.3.27*, 18.7.27, *20.7.27*, 23.7.27, 8.1.28,
    20.1.28, 27.1.28, 8.2.28, 9.3.28, 7.6.28, 2.8.28, 4.9.28.
Shrew Mouse, Pigmy (Pygmy Shrew) *29.8.27*.
Squirrel, Red *26.1.28*, 24.9.28.
Squirrels 10.6.27, 25.6.27, 4.2.28.
Stoat 24.2.27, 15.7.28.
Weasel *24.2.27*, 6.12.27.

## OTHER ANIMALS

Ant, Common Brown Garden (Red Ant) *27.10.26*, 15.7.28.
Bee (Honey Bee) 23.11.26, 26.2.28.
Beetle, Great Diving 1.8.28; Tiger *5.5.28*.
Beetle (Wasp Beetle) *26.5.28*, (Great Diving Beetle) 29.7.28.
Beetles *24.11.26*, 17.3.27, *22.5.27*, *30.6.27*, *20.10.27*, *30.5.28*,
    11.6.28, 22.6.28
Butterfly, Brimstone *10.4.27*, 3.10.27, 6.10.27, 26.3.28; Clifton
    Blue (Adonis Blue) *5.8.27*; Common Blue *5.8.27*, 29.5.28,
    1.8.28; Dingey Skipper (Dingy Skipper) *19.5.28*, 25.5.28;
    Gatekeeper (recorded by author as Large Heath, a name
    now used for a different species) *2.8.28*; Green-veined
    White 29.5.28; Grizzled Skipper *3.7.27*, 25.5.28; Large
    White *5.8.27*, 25.5.28, 26.7.28; Meadow Brown *27.6.27*,
    10.7.28, 17.7.28, 26.7.28; Painted Lady 30.5.28; Peacock
    5.8.27, 1.9.27, 15.10.27, 26.4.28, 26.7.28, 6.8.28; Purple
    Emperor 17.7.28; Red Admiral *25.8.27*, 27.9.27, 6.10.27,
    11.9.28; Ringlet *30.7.28*; Small Heath *29.5.28*, 1.6.28, 26.7.28;
    Small Tortoiseshell *5.11.26*, 7.11.26, 20.12.26, 2.8.27, 5.8.27,
    6.10.27, 3.11.27, 6.8.28, 31.8.28; Small White *26.4.28*,
    25.5.28, 26.7.28, 31.7.28; Speckled Wood *27.9.28*;
    Wall (Wall Brown) *16.8.27*; Yellow Brimstone (Brimstone)
    17.9.28.
Caddis worm (Caddis fly larva) *21.1.28*.
Caterpillar, Looper 2.8.28.
Centipede (millipede) 19.3.27.
Centipede 13.5.28.
Cockchafer 27.5.28, 4.6.28.
Cockles 25.7.27.
Crane flies / Daddy long-legs *27.9.27*, 7.5.28.
Crustaceans *31.8.28*.
Dragonflies 3.8.27, 25.5.28, 27.5.28, *21.7.28*, 22.7.28, 26.7.28,
    29.7.28, 6.8.28, 5.9.28.
Earwig *16.8.27*, 27.12.27, 13.10.28.
Fish 25.7.27, 7.1.28, 17.6.28, 23.7.28, 21.12.28.
Fly, Bluebottle 7.11.26, 20.12.26, 5.11.27, 19.1.28; Common
    Drone *7.11.26*; House 7.11.26.
Frog (Common Frog) *3.3.27*, *13.3.27*, *17.3.27*, 20.3.27, *22.3.27*,
    1.4.27, 6.4.27, 8.4.27, 18.6.27, 28.8.27, 2.9.27, 8.2.28, *18.2.28*,
    23.2.28, 25.2.28, 26.2.28, 18.3.28, 19.5.28, 9.7.28, *22.7.28*,
    26.7.28, 29.7.28, 18.8.28.
Gall, Artichoke *21.1.28*; Marble *21.1.28*; Oak Apple 21.1.28,
    22.1.28, 19.5.28; Robin's Pincushion 2.10.28.
Goldfish 24.11.26, 3.11.27, 23.7.28, 1.8.28, 10.11.28.
Grasshopper, Common English Meadow (Meadow
    Grasshopper) 2.9.27.
Grasshoppers 29.7.28.
Grubs, insect *17.11.27*, 13.5.28.
Harvesters (Harvestmen) 29.7.28.
Hornet 2.6.27.
Humble bee (Bumblebee) 3.3.27, *11.9.27*.
Ladybird, Seven-spotted (7-Spot Ladybird) 21.4.27, 15.9.28;
    Two-spotted (2-Spot Ladybird) *21.4.27*, 14.9.28.
Limpets *31.8.28*.
Lizards 8.6.28, 9.6.28, 14.6.28, 18.6.28.
Midges 26.2.28.
Minnow 24.1.28.
Mosquito, Common / Common Gnat 4.10.27, 7.5.28.
Moth, Angle Shades *18.9.28*; Cinnabar *29.7.28*, 9.8.28; Herald
    9.9.27, *19–20.9.28*; Large Red-belted Clearwing (Red-belted
    Clearwing) 27.5.28; Plume *21.10.27*; Triple Spotted Clay
    *30.7.28*; White Ermine *3.9.27*, 10.5.28; White-pinion Spotted
    *25.5.28*; Winter 30.10.27, *13.11.28*, 6.12.28.
Moths 22.11.27, 17.12.28.
Newts 8.4.27, 1.8.28.
Pond Skater *22.4.27*, 27.5.28.
Slugs 27.1.27, 1.4.27.
Snail (Banded Snail) *1.12.26*; (Garden Snail) 1.12.26.

Spiders *6.8.27*, 2.9.27, 9.9.27, *19.9.27*, 17.11.27, 13.5.28.
Toad (Common Toad) 24.11.26, 17.3.27, *1.4.27*, 29.5.28, 18.8.28, 14.11.28; Natterjack 27.5.28.
Wasps *5.11.26*, 25.4.27, *6.8.27*, 16.8.27, 7.9.27, 4.10.27, 6.10.27, 14.10.27, 3.11.27, 27.4.28, 13.5.28, 17.7.28, 2.8.28, 1.9.28, 5.9.28, 15.9.28, 3.10.28, 15.10.28, 17.11.28; Gall 2.10.28; Solitary 13.9.28.
Winkles *31.8.28*.
Worms (Earthworms) 27.10.26, 17.3.27, 30.4.27, 7.11.27, 13.11.27, 12.12.27, *14.5.28*, 1.7.28, 25.7.28, 27.7.28, 16.9.28.

## PLANTS

Accacias (acacias) 5.6.28.
Aconite *27.1.26*, 8.1.28, 28.1.28.
Agrimony, Common (Agrimony) 2.9.27.
Almond *22.3.27*, *23.3.27*, 25.3.28.
Anchusa 24.6.28.
Anemone, Wood 6.3.28, 25.3.28, 23.4.28.
Anthrinum (Antirhinum) 22.10.26.
Antirrhinum 7.12.26, 16.12.26, 27.5.28.
Apple 21.3.27, 8.10.27, 22.11.27, 19.1.28, 27.1.28, 20.6.28, 1.7.28, 2.7.28, 5.7.28 (in journal as 5.6.28), 22.7.28, 15.9.28, 11.10.28, 28.12.28.
Arabis 1.3.27, 22.3.27, 30.5.27, 6.2.28.
Ash *17.12.27*, 1.5.28, 13.5.28, 21.7.28, 20.9.28, 18.11.28.
Aubretia (Aubrieta) 1.3.27, 22.3.27, 30.5.27, 5.2.28, 14.2.28, 23.3.28.
Avens, Common/'Herb Bennet' (Herb Bennet) 15.5.28; Water 9.5.27.
Bamboos 21.4.28.
Barley 25.7.28, 20.6.28.
Bedstraw, Crosswort (Crosswort) 6.5.28; Hedge 6.6.28; Yellow (Lady's Bedstraw) 16.6.28, 10.8.28; Water (Fen or Marsh Bedstraw?) 24.6.28.
Beech *22.10.26*, 23.7.27, 22.10.27, 31.10.27, 9.12.27, 14.2.28, 27.3.28, 8.4.28, 1.5.28, 18.6.28, 7.10.28.
Bellflower, Nettle-leaved 31.7.28.
Bindweed, Great/Greater (Large Bindweed) *7.7.27*, 14.7.28, 27.7.28, 11.9.28; Lesser/Small (Bindweed, Field Bindweed) *10.8.27*, 12.6.28, 14.7.28, 19.8.28.
Birch, Silver/Birch (Silver Birch) 7.1.28, 24.1.28, 18.11.28, 29.12.28.
Blackberry (Bramble) 28.8.27, 2.9.27, 6.6.28.
Blackthorn 23.3.27, 2.4.28.
Bluebell 13.3.27, 10.2.28, 27.3.28, 5.5.28, 29.7.28; Scotch (Harebell) 29.7.28.
Bracken 7.10.27, 5.5.28, 10.10.28.
Bramble 24.2.27, 11.3.27, 9.12.27, 31.12.27.
Brooklime 9.6.28.
Broom/Common Broom/Yellow Broom/15.7.27, 16.7.27, 12.6.28, 14.6.28, 16.6.28.
Broom, Sweet-scented (Spanish Broom) 16.6.28.
Broomrape, Greater 11.6.28.
Bryony, Black *20.5.28*; White 12.11.27, 7.8.28.
Buddlea (Buddleia) 11.7.27.
Bugle/Bugle, Common 27.4.27, 29.4.28.
Bugloss, Viper's *11.8.27*, 28.8.27, 11.6.28, 10.8.28.
Bullrush (Bulrush, Reedmace) 3.6.27, 22.7.28.
Burdock 2.8.28.
Buttercup, Bulbous *11.5.28*, 21.12.28; Meadow/ 'Upright Crowfoot' (Meadow Buttercup) 7.5.28, 11.5.28.
Buttercups 8.5.27, 15.7.27, 12.11.27, 16.5.28.
Cabbage 19.8.28.
Cactus (*Opuntia*) 12.6.28, 13.6.28.
Camelia *10.4.27*, 1.4.28.
Campanula *16.12.26*, 22.5.27, 12.6.28, 21.12.28.

Campion, Bladder 9.6.28, 17.7.28; Pink (Red Campion) 9.5.27, 23.4.28, 16.5.28, 4.6.28, 26.11.28; White *2.8.27*, 4.6.28; White Evening (White Campion? Night-flowering Catchfly?) 1.6.28.
Campions 31.10.28.
Canterbury Bells 24.6.28.
Catmint 30.5.27.
Cat's-ear, Long-rooted (Cat's-ear) 27.6.28.
Celandine (Lesser Celandine) 12.3.28.
Centauria, Common (Common Centaury) 14.6.28, 17.7.28.
Cerastium 30.5.27.
Chamomile, Common (Corn Chamomile) 29.7.28; Rayless (Rayless or Pineapple Mayweed) 1.8.28.
Charlock 7.10.28.
Cherry 20.6.28; Wild 16.10.27, 4.4.28.
Chestnut 12.3.27, 2.6.27, 7.10.27, 16.10.27, 10.4.28, 23.9.28, 6.10.28.
Chestnut, Horse 8.5.27, 9.10.27, 27.7.28; Spanish (Sweet Chestnut) *10.2.28*, 27.3.28, 18.6.28.
Chicory 14.6.28.
Chrysanthemum 22.10.26, *24.11.26*, 13.10.27.
Cinquefoil, Creeping 4.6.27, 14.6.28.
Clematis *20.12.26*, 2.6.27, 9.9.27, 16.10.27, 19.2.28.
Clovers 19.6.28, 22.6.28.
Clover, Common Purple or Red (Red Clover) 9.5.28, 21.6.28; White/Clover, White Dutch (White Clover) 17.7.27, 20.7.27, 5.6.28, 19.6.28, 21.6.28.
Comfrey, Common 9.6.28.
Convolvulus 16.6.28; (*Convolvulus lineatus*?) *14.6.28*.
Convolvulus, Pink (Mallow-leaved Bindweed) *13–14.6.28*.
Corn (Wheat) 10.5.27, *26.7.27*, 22.6.28.
Corn Cockle *19–22.6.28*.
Cornflower 19.6.28, 20.6.28, 21.6.28.
*Coronilla varia* (Crown Vetch) 9.6.28.
Cotton grass 16.6.28.
Cowslip 3.3.28, 25.3.28, 14.4.28.
Crane's Bill, Dove's Foot (Round-leaved Crane's Bill?) 19.5.28, 9.6.28; Meadow 16.7.27.
Creeper, Virginia 7.9.27, 22.7.28, 9.10.28.
Cress, Wart (Greater Celandine) 5.4.28.
Crocus *1.3.27*, 3.3.27, 22.3.27, 8.1.28, 28.1.28, 1.2.28, 6.2.28.
Cuckoo Flower/'Lady's Smock' (Cuckooflower) 5.4.28.
Cuckoo Pint (Lords-and-ladies) 18.4.28.
Cudweed, Marsh 4.10.28.
Cypress 12.6.28.
Daffodil, 20.12.26, 22.3.27, 28.1.28, 3.3.28.
Dahlia 22.10.26, 13.10.27, 2.11.27, 11.11.27, 15.7.28.
Daisy, Common (Daisy) 7.3.28, 26.11.28; Michaelmas 27.9.27, 13.10.27; Ox-eye 15.7.27, 4.6.28, 5.6.28, 22.6.28, 15.7.28.
Dandelion 9.3.28, 29.4.28, 12.6.28.
Dead-nettle, Spotted 8.6.28, 14.6.28; White 15.4.28, 30.10.28; Yellow (Yellow Archangel) 3.5.28.
Delphinium 24.6.28.
Dodder, Lesser (Common Dodder) 2.8.28.
Dogwood 10.10.28.
Duckweed, Lesser 5.7.28 (in journal as 5.6.28).
Elder 17.9.28, 18.9.28, 19.9.28.
Elms *17.3.27*, 26.7.27, 8.3.28, 27.5.28, 19.8.28, 7.10.28, 18.11.28.
*Erica carnea* (Winter Heath) 5.2.28.
Eucalyptus 10.5.27.
Eyebright, Common/'Wild Basil' (Common Eyebright) 31.7.28, 2.8.28.
Fennel, Common (Fennel) 27.7.28.
Fern, Polly Polly (Polypody Fern) 21.1.28.
Figwort (Common Figwort) 6.7.28 (in journal as 6.6.28).
Firs 17.9.27, 12.6.28, 18.11.28, 29.12.28.
Flag, Yellow (Yellow Iris) 29.5.28; Common 14.6.28; Slender-leaved (Pale Flax) 11.6.28, 16.6.28.

Fleabane (Common Fleabane) 28.7.28, 2.8.28.
Forget-me-not 1.4.27, 6.5.28; Water 24.6.28.
Foxglove 15.7.27, 28.5.28, 4.6.28.
Frankia 30.5.27.
Fumitory, Common 14.5.28.
Geranium 22.10.26, 1.6.27.
Geum 30.5.27.
Golden Rod (Goldenrod) 20.9.28.
Goosefoot, White (Fat Hen) 31.7.28.
Gorse, Dwarf/Dwarf Furze (Dwarf Gorse) 27.9.28.
Grasses 14.6.28, 22.6.28.
Grass, Couch *20.12.26*; Quaking 6.6.28.
Ground-Elder/'Goutweed' (Ground-Elder) 1.7.28.
Groundsel 7.3.28, 21.12.28.
Gunnera 14.4.28.
Harebell 22.5.27, 17.7.28, 29.7.28, 31.7.28.
Hawkbit, Hairy (Rough Hawkbit) 27.6.28; Rough 1.6.28.
Hawkweed 30.10.28.
Hawthorn 4.9.28, 19.9.28, 29.12.28.
Hazel *2.9.27*, *12.11.27*, 1.12.27, *8.2.28*, 8.4.28.
Heartsease 16.7.27.
Heather, Bell 16.7.27, *22.7.27*, 7.6.28; Cross-leaved
    (Cross-leaved Heath) *22.7.27*; Ling (Heather) 15.7.27,
    22.7.27, 5.5.28, 2.8.28.
Helleborine (Broad-leaved Helleborine) 28.7.28.
Hepatica 22.3.27.
Herb Robert *27.4.27*, 31.10.28.
Hogweed 30.10.28.
Holly 25.10.26, *21.11.26*, *23.11.26*, 1.12.26, 11.6.27, 19.6.27,
    13.11.27, 1.12.27, 12.12.27, 23.12.27, 27.12.27, 16.1.28,
    ·27.4.28, 7.7.28 (in journal as 7.6.28), 16.9.28, 3.10.28,
    18.11.28.
Hollyhock 26.7.27.
Honeysuckle 19.6.27, 10.2.28, 5.6.28, 12.6.28, 14.9.28.
Hop/Common Hop (Hop) 9.5.27, 7.8.28, 27.9.28.
Horse tails (horsetails) 22.4.28.
Hyacinth 27.1.27, 1.3.27, 22.3.27, 23.3.27, 25.2.28, 3.3.28,
    11.3.28, 23.3.28; Grape 22.3.27, 16.1.28, 19.1.28, 23.3.28.
*Ilex* (Holly) 15.5.27.
Iris, cultivated 10.5.27, 15.5.27, 5.2.28.
Iris, Purple Flag 9.5.27; Yellow/Iris, Yellow Flag (Yellow Iris)
    10.5.27, 4.6.27, 3.6.28.
Ivy 8.4.27, *5.11.27*, 17.12.27, 11.1.28, 7.2.28, 21.4.28, 27.4.28,
    5.9.28, 9.10.28, 10.10.28, 18.11.28; Ground 10.4.27, 19.3.28,
    23.4.28, 28.12.28.
'Jack-by-the-Hedge' (Garlic Mustard) 5.5.28.
*Jasminum nudiflorum* (Winter Jasmine) 22.11.27.
Kapweed [Knapweed] (Red Star-Thistle) *14.6.28*; Black
    (Common Knapweed, Hardheads) *3.7.27*, 30.10.28.
Knot Grass (Knotgrass) 12.10.28.
Laburnum 8.5.27.
Larch 23.3.28, 1.4.28.
Laurel 30.12.27, *8.2.28*, 8.4.28, 27.4.28, 4.12.28; Lettuce, Wall
    26.6.28, 27.6.28.
Lilac 19.3.28, 29.4.28.
Lilies/water-lilies (water-lilies) 24.11.26, 22.4.27, 15.7.27,
    3.11.27, 17.12.27, 7.1.28, 14.4.28, 27.5.28, 8.7.28, 22.7.28,
    26.7.28, 6.8.28, 5.9.28.
Lily, Lenten (Wild Daffodil) *26.3.27*.
*Linum flavum* (Yellow Flax) 8.5.27, 30.5.27.
*Linum perenne* (Dwarf Flax) 30.5.27.
Lithospermum *22.12.26*, 30.5.27.
Lobelia 22.10.26.
Lupin 30.5.27, 16.7.27, 24.6.28.
Mallow, Common 15.6.28; Musk 11.7.27, 14.7.28; Pink
    (Common Mallow?) 10.5.27 .
Mangles (Mangelwurzels) 20.3.27.
Maple 18.6.28.

Marguerite (Marguerite Daisy) 27.10.26.
Marigolds 22.6.28.
Marigold, Marsh 28.3.28, 14.4.28.
Marjoram, Common (Marjoram) 27.7.28, 31.7.28.
May (Hawthorn) 26.4.27, 8.5.27, 16.7.27, 7.9.27, *16.12.27*,
    20.2.28, 13.5.28, 16.5.28.
Mayweed, Scentless 4.10.28.
Meadow Sweet (Meadowsweet) 23.5.27, 11.7.27, 16.6.28,
    19.7.28.
Medick, Black 18.5.28.
Milkwort, Blue (Common Milkwort or maybe Heath Milkwort)
    5.5.28; White (Common Milkwort) 5.5.28.
Mint, Corn 29.7.28; Hairy (Water Mint) 29.7.28.
Moschatel 23.4.28.
Mosses 23.12.27, 21.1.28, 1.4.28.
Mulberry (Black Mulberry) 2.8.27.
Mullein, Great/Verbascum (Great Mullein) 8.6.28.
Mustard 9.5.27, 19.6.28, 21.6.28, 14.7.28, 10.10.28.
Narcissus 27.1.27, 22.3.27, 28.1.28, 9.6.28.
Nasturtium 10.5.27, 3.10.27.
Nettle, Stinging 3.6.28.
Nightshade, Common Enchanter's (Enchanter's Nightshade)
    9.7.28; Woody or Bittersweet (Bittersweet) *6.7.28*
    (in journal as 6.6.28), 11.8.28.
Nipplewort 26.6.28, 27.6.28.
Oak (Pedunculate Oak) *2.9.27*, 12.11.27, 1.12.27, 11.1.28,
    15.1.28, *21.1.28*, 11.2.28, 1.5.28, 27.5.28, 11.7.28, 2.8.28,
    4.9.28, 6.10.28, 14.11.28, 17.11.28, 18.11.28, 19.12.28.
Oats 25.7.27, 6.6.28, 14.7.28, 4.9.28.
Old Man's Beard (Traveller's Joy) 11.9.28.
Olive 12.6.28.
Orange 10.5.27.
Orchid, Common Purple (Early Purple Orchid).
Orchis (orchid) 16.6.28.
Orchis, Bee (Bee Orchid) 16.6.28; Early Purple (Early Purple
    Orchid) 28.4.27, *29.4.27*, 9.5.28; Pyramidal (Pyramidal
    Orchid) 12.6.28; Spotted (Common Spotted Orchid) 4.6.27,
    4.6.28, 8.6.28.
'Palm' (Goat Willow) 2.3.27, 11.2.28, 10.3.28.
Palms 15.5.27.
Parsley (Cow Parsley) 11.7.27, 5.5.28, 16.5.28; Hedge
    (probably Upright Hedge-Parsley) 24.6.28.
Parsnip, Wild 31.7.28.
Pea, Everlasting (Broad-leaved Everlasting Pea) 14.6.28;
    Narrow-leaved Everlasting 8.6.28; Sweet 31.7.28.
Pear 17.10.27, 15.9.28, 11.10.28.
Periwinkle 22.3.27.
Persicaria, Climbing/Convolvulus Knotgrass 15.7.28;
    Spotted 17.7.28.
'Pig Nut' (Pignut) 3.5.28.
Pimpernel, Scarlet 8.6.28; Yellow/Wood Loosestrife
    (Yellow Pimpernel) 10.5.28, 29.5.28.
Pine, Umbrella (Stone Pine) 6.6.28.
Pines 3.10.27, 24.1.28, 5.3.28, *7.6.28*, 6.10.28.
Pink (Common Pink) 30.5.27, 24.6.28.
Plane 25.10.26, 9.10.27, 16.6.28.
Plantain, Water/Alisma (Common Water-Plantain) 17.7.28.
Plum 26.6.27, 6.11.27, 5.12.27, 18.3.28, 16.9.28; Japanese
    25.3.28; Wild 23.3.27, 13.3.28.
Poplar, White 6.9.28.
Poplars 10.5.27, 7.10.27, 9.10.27.
Poppies 15.11.27, 9.6.28, 16.6.28, 19.6.28, 20.6.28, 21.6.28,
    22.6.28, 31.7.28.
Poppy/Poppy, Common Red (Common Poppy) 10.5.27,
    2.7.27, *23.7.27*, 4.6.28, 5.6.28; Oriental 30.5.27, 16.7.27,
    24.6.28; Shirley 9.6.28; Yellow Horned *19.8.27*, 10.8.28.
Potato 26.7.27, 19.6.28.
Potentilla 4.7.27.

143

Primrose 27.1.26, 3.3.27, *13.3.27*, 26.3.27, 8.1.28, 25.1.28, 8.2.28, 10.2.28, 23.4.28, 28.12.28; cultivated *22.12.26*; Evening 6.7.27.
*Primula denticulata* 16.12.26.
Privet 5.6.28, 7.10.28.
*Pyrus japonica* 22.11.27.
Ragged Robin 15.5.28.
Ragwort (Common Ragwort) 27.7.28, *29.7.28*, 30.7.28, 31.7.28, 2.8.28, 30.10.28; Marsh 27.6.28.
Rape 28.12.28.
Rattle, Yellow 11.6.28, 12.6.28.
Reed, Common 3.6.28.
Rest Harrow (Common Rest Harrow) 14.7.27, 31.7.28, 2.8.28; (Large Yellow Rest Harrow) 14.6.28.
Rhododendron 16.7.27.
Rock-rose, Yellow (Common Rock-rose) 16.7.27, 7.6.28.
Rock-roses 8.5.27, 30.5.27, 14.2.28, 12.6.28, 16.6.28.
Rose, Christmas (Black Hellebore) 27.1.27, 8.1.28, 28.1.28.
Roses, cultivated 22.10.26, 28.11.26, *7.12.26*, 10.5.27, 15.5.27, 30.5.27, 2.6.27, 19.9.27, 13.10.27, 16.10.27, 12.11.27, 19.2.28, 7.7.28 (in journal as 7.6.28), 18.9.28.
Rose, Guelder 31.7.28; Wild (including Dog Rose) 10.5.27, 22.5.27, *15.6.27*, 3.7.27, 15.7.27, 30.5.28, 5.6.28, 2.10.28.
Rosebay (Rosebay Willowherb) 14.7.28, 19.7.28, 2.8.28.
Rowan 31.7.28, 10.10.28.
Sage, Meadow 6.6.28, 20.6.28.
Sainfoin 20.6.28.
St John's Wort, Square-stemmed (Square-stalked St John's Wort) 9.7.28.
Sallow/'Palm' (Goat Willow) 8.2.28, 20.2.28, 26.4.28.
Sandwort, 3 Nerved (Three-veined Sandwort) 3.5.28.
Sanicle, Wood (Sanicle) 26.4.28.
Santolina (Lavender Cotton) *14.6.28*.
*Saponaria* (soapworts) 22.5.27, 30.5.27.
*Saponaria ocymoides* (Rock Soapwort) 12.6.28.
'Saxifrage, Tuberous'/'Pretty Maids' 9.6.28.
Scabious 9.6.28; Field 5.6.28, 14.7.28, 31.7.28; Small *11.9.27*, 29.7.28.
Scilla 1.3.27, 22.3.27, 5.2.28, 3.3.28.
Self-Heal 26.6.28.
Silverweed 5.7.28 (in journal as 5.6.28).
Snakeweed (Common Bistort) 9.6.28.
Sneezewort 29.7.28.
'Snow Berries' (Snowberry) 10.10.28.
Snowdrop 19.1.27, 22.12.27, 8.1.28, 28.1.28.
Sorrel, Red (Pink Oxalis) 16.6.28; Upright Yellow Wood (Upright Yellow Sorrel) 5.7.28 (in journal as 5.6.28); Wood 10.4.27, 9.4.28, 23.4.28.
Sow-thistle, Common/Milk Thistle (could be Smooth, Perennial or Prickly Sow-thistles) 1.6.28, 30.10.28.
Spearwort, Lesser 26.6.28.
Speedwell, Common (Common Field Speedwell) 3.5.28; Field 2.4.28; Germander 1.5.28; Ivy-leaved 19.3.28.
Spirea, Spireia (Spiraea) 28.11.26, 16.12.26, 11.11.27, 19.11.27, 22.11.27, 18.12.27, *8.2.28*, 22.7.28, 22.11.28, 25.11.28, 4.12.28, 9.12.28, 10.12.28, 11.12.28, 12.12.28, 16.12.28, 18.12.28, 21.12.28.
Spleenwort, Maidenhair 8.6.28, *9.10.28*; Wallrue (Wall-rue) 11.6.28, 9.10.28, 9.10.28.
Spruce 20.2.28.
Spurge, Petty 27.9.28.
Stitchwort, Greater *27.4.27*, 12.4.28, 15.4.28; Lesser 24.6.28.
Stock 22.10.26, 16.12.26, *22.12.26*.
Stonecrop 6.6.28.
Storks Bill, Hemlock (Musk Storksbill?) 5.6.28.
Strawberry, Wild *27.10.26*, 22.5.27, 6.3.28, 8.6.28.
Sunflower 6.9.28.
Sycamore 25.6.28.

Tamarisk 4.6.28.
Tansy *20–21.8.28*.
Teasle (Teasel) 6.6.28.
Tea-Tree, Duke of Argyll's 11.8.28.
Thistle, Dwarf Plume (Dwarf Thistle) 31.7.28; Marsh Plume (Marsh Thistle) *11.8.27*; Musk/Thistle, Nodding (Musk Thistle) 9.6.28, 20.6.28; Scotch (Spear Thistle) 5.6.28, 6.6.28; Spear Plume (Spear Thistle) 18.7.28, 27.7.28, 2.8.28.; White Plume (probably Meadow Thistle) 24.6.28.
Thistles 13.6.28, 16.6.28.
Thorn (Hawthorn) 25.10.26, 4.3.28, 23.3.28, 26.3.28, 7.10.28.
Thrift 14.7.27.
Thyme 14.7.27, 17.6.28.
Thyme, creeping (*Thymus longicaulis*) 16.6.28.
Toadflax, Ivy-leaved 29.5.28, 8.6.28, 9.10.28; Yellow (Common Toadflax) 31.7.28.
Tormentil 8.6.28, 14.9.28.
Traveller's Joy *27.4.28*.
Tree, Cork (Cork Oak) *7.6.28*; Wayfaring 31.7.28, 19.8.28.
Trefoil, Bird's-Foot 14.7.27, 19.5.28, 29.5.28; Hop 4.6.27, 7.5.28; Marsh Bird's-Foot (Greater Bird's-Foot Trefoil) 4.10.28.
Tulips *24.11.26*, 27.1.27, 1.3.27, 30.5.27, 28.1.28.
Turnip 26.7.27, 11.10.28.
Valerian, Red/Valerian (Red Valerian) 23.5.27, 5.6.28.
Verbascum (Mullein) 9.8.28.
Veronica 10.5.27, 21.12.28.
Vetch, Hairy (Hairy Tare) 25.5.28; Tufted 5.6.28.
Vetches 22.5.27, 11.7.27, 11.6.28.
Vetchling, Meadow 12.6.28, 26.6.28.
Vine, Grape 10.5.27, 5.6.28, 19.6.28.
Violas 9.6.28.
Violet, Dog *10.4.27*, 28.8.27, 27.3.28, 1.4.28, 23.4.28; Sweet 9.3.28; White 26.3.27, 11.3.28.
Violets 26.2.28, 4.3.28.
Wallflower 21.12.28.
Walnut 2.7.28, 5.7.28 (in journal as 5.6.28), 8.7.28.
Watercress 6.10.28.
Water-Lily, Yellow 14.7.28.
Water-Lillies, White (White Water Lily) 5.6.28.
Wheat 15.7.27, 25.7.27, 19.6.28, 21.6.28, 14.7.28, 31.7.28, 19.8.28.
Willow Herb, Greater/Great Hairy (Great Willowherb) 3.6.28, 14.7.28; Small-flowered Hairy (Small-flowered Willowherb) 24.6.28; Rose Bay (Rosebay Willowherb) 27.6.28.
Willow herbs (willowherbs) 11.9.28.
Willow, Pussy (Goat Willow) *2.3.27*.
Willows 7.10.28.
Wistaria (Wisteria) 1.5.27, 27.4.28, 12.10.28
Wood Rush, Field 14.4.28.
Woundwort, Hedge 24.6.28, 2.8.28.
Yarrow 14.7.27, 7.6.28, 29.7.28; Pink (pink-flowered form of Yarrow) 19.8.28, 20.8.28.
Yew 28.11.26, *21.1.28*, 13.2.28, 21.4.28, 6.8.28.

# FUNGI, LICHENS, SEAWEEDS
Candle Snuff fungus 21.1.28.
*Chlorosplenium* fungus 22.1.28.
Fungi *28.8.27*.
Lichen, Reindeer ('Reindeer Moss') 21.1.28.
Lichens 23.12.27, 11.1.28, 21.1.28, 27.3.28.
Mould, cotton wool 28.8.27.
Pixy Cup lichen *21.1.28*.
Puff ball 28.8.27.
Sea Wrack, Knotty (Knotted Wrack) *18.8.27*.
Toadstools *28.8.27*, 2.9.27.
Tree Beard lichen *21.1.28*.
*Tremella* fungus 21.1.28